Montréal and Quebec City Travel Guide

The Ultimate Guide to Hidden Gems and Cultural Experiences - A Curated Adventure Through Historic Landmarks and Breathtakins

Tom Tremblay

information is without contract or any type of guarantee assurance.

The trademarks that are used are without any consent, and the publication of the trademark is without permission or backing by the trademark owner. All trademarks and brands within this book are for clarifying purposes only and are the owned by the owners themselves, not affiliated with this document.

TABLE OF CONTENTS

INTRODUCTION: WHY MONTREAL AND QUEBEC CITY?

The Allure of French-Canadian Culture

Embracing the essence of French-Canadian culture is akin to stepping into a vibrant tapestry woven with threads of history, language, artistry, and culinary delights. This unique cultural amalgamation finds its roots deeply embedded in the 17th century, when French explorers and settlers first set foot on the shores of what is now Quebec. Over the centuries, this cultural heritage has flourished, nurturing a distinctive identity that is both proudly French and unmistakably Canadian.

In the streets of Montreal and Quebec City, the French language forms the cornerstone of daily life, infusing these urban landscapes with a distinctive European flair. The melodic cadence of French spoken by locals is not just a means of communication but an embodiment of cultural pride. Street signs, menus, and even casual conversations remind visitors that they are in a place where French is not only preserved but celebrated. This linguistic legacy extends beyond verbal interactions, permeating art, literature, and music, where French-Canadian artists contribute a unique voice to the global cultural dialogue.

The architectural landscape of these cities is a testament to their rich history. In Old Montreal and Old Quebec, cobblestone streets and stone buildings transport visitors back in time. These historic districts are peppered with structures dating back to the 17th and 18th centuries, each narrating stories of the past. The Notre-Dame Basilica in Montreal, with its intricate Gothic Revival architecture, and the Château Frontenac in Quebec City, standing majestically over the St. Lawrence River, are iconic symbols of this enduring heritage. These landmarks are not merely tourist attractions; they are living museums that echo the stories of those who walked these streets centuries ago.

Art and creativity flow freely through the veins of French-Canadian culture. Montreal, often hailed as a cultural capital, hosts a plethora of festivals and events that celebrate artistic expression in all its forms. The Montreal Jazz Festival and the Just for Laughs Festival are world-renowned, drawing artists and audiences from across the globe. In Quebec City, the Fête de la Nouvelle-France pays homage to the region's historical roots with vibrant reenactments and celebrations. These festivals are a reflection of the French-Canadian spirit, one that embraces creativity and revels in communal celebration.

Culinary experiences in these regions offer a delectable journey through French-Canadian culture. The cuisine is a flavorful fusion of French culinary techniques and local ingredients, resulting in dishes that are both comforting and sophisticated. Poutine, a beloved Quebecois creation, combines crispy fries, cheese curds, and savory gravy, offering a taste of indulgence. Tourtière, a meat pie traditionally served during the holiday season, is another staple that showcases the region's culinary ingenuity. In Montreal, the Jewish community introduced the world to the Montreal-style bagel and smoked meat, both of which have become integral to the city's culinary identity. These dishes, alongside countless others, invite visitors to savor the unique flavors that define French-Canadian gastronomy.

French-Canadian culture is also characterized by its strong sense of community and tradition. The warmth and hospitality of the locals create an inviting atmosphere where visitors are made to feel like part of the family. Music, dance, and storytelling are integral to community gatherings, where traditional folk songs and dances such as the "gigue" are passed down through generations. These communal activities are more than just entertainment; they are a means of preserving and perpetuating cultural traditions.

Nature and the environment hold a special place in French-Canadian culture, influencing lifestyle and leisure activities. The landscape, with its sprawling forests, majestic rivers, and picturesque mountains, provides a stunning backdrop for outdoor pursuits. In winter, snow-covered terrains become playgrounds for skiing, snowshoeing, and ice skating, while summer offers opportunities for hiking, kayaking, and camping. The changing seasons are celebrated with gusto, as they bring with them a host of activities and festivals that showcase the harmonious relationship between people and nature.

Religion, too, has played a significant role in shaping French-Canadian culture. Catholicism, introduced by early settlers, has left an indelible mark on the cultural fabric, influencing architecture, traditions, and community values. Historic churches and religious festivals remain important aspects of cultural life, serving as reminders of the region's spiritual heritage.

The resilience and adaptability of French-Canadian culture are evident in its ability to honor tradition while embracing modernity. As new influences and global trends emerge, the culture evolves, blending the old with the new in a dynamic dance that continues to captivate and inspire. The preservation of local traditions alongside the acceptance of contemporary influences ensures that French-Canadian culture remains vibrant and relevant.

Ultimately, the allure of French-Canadian culture lies in its harmonious blend of history, language, art, and community spirit. It is a culture that invites exploration and participation, offering a rich tapestry of experiences that leave an indelible mark on those who immerse themselves in it. Whether through the beauty of its landscapes, the warmth of its people, or the richness of its artistic expressions, French-Canadian culture captivates the heart and mind, offering a unique and unforgettable journey into the soul of Quebec.

Brief History of Montreal and Quebec City

Montreal and Quebec City, two jewels of French-Canada, boast a rich tapestry of history that has shaped their identities over centuries. Their stories are deeply interwoven with the broader narrative of European exploration and settlement in North America, with each city offering its own unique glimpse into the past, marked by resilience, transformation, and cultural fusion.

The origins of Montreal trace back to the early 17th century, when the island was first encountered by French explorer Jacques Cartier in 1535. He noted the presence of a large indigenous settlement, Hochelaga, at the foot of Mount Royal. However, it wasn't until 1642 that the city of Montreal, initially named Ville-Marie, was officially founded by Paul Chomedey de Maisonneuve and Jeanne Mance. Their mission was both religious and colonial, aiming to convert Indigenous peoples to Christianity and establish a French foothold in the New World. The settlement faced numerous challenges, from harsh winters to conflicts with Iroquois nations, but its strategic location along the St. Lawrence River ensured its growth as a hub for trade, particularly in fur.

By the 18th century, Montreal had evolved into a bustling port city, vital for commerce and military strategy. The city's fortunes shifted dramatically in 1760 during the French and Indian War, when British forces captured Montreal, marking the end of French rule in Canada. This transition brought about significant changes, as British governance introduced new legal systems and economic practices. Despite these transformations, the French-speaking population retained their language and religion, laying the foundation for the city's bilingual and bicultural character.

Quebec City, founded in 1608 by Samuel de Champlain, is one of North America's oldest cities. Its strategic location on a cliff overlooking the St. Lawrence River made it an ideal military and trading post. Champlain's settlement, initially a small fort and trading post, grew over time into the administrative center of New France. The city's fortifications, including the famed Citadelle, are a testament to its military significance, designed to protect against British invasions.

The 1759 Battle of the Plains of Abraham was a pivotal moment in Quebec City's history. British forces, led by General James Wolfe, defeated the French troops commanded by Marquis de Montcalm, leading to British control of New France. The battle was brief but decisive, with both commanding generals dying from wounds sustained in the conflict. The Treaty of Paris in 1763 formalized the transfer of power, and Quebec became a British colony. Despite this change, the British allowed the French-speaking inhabitants to retain their language, religion, and civil laws, a decision that has profoundly influenced Quebec's cultural landscape.

Throughout the 19th century, both Montreal and Quebec City experienced waves of immigration, industrialization, and urbanization. Montreal emerged as Canada's economic powerhouse, driven by industries like textiles, railways, and finance. Its diverse population swelled with immigrants from Ireland, Scotland, and later Eastern Europe, each group contributing to the city's multicultural mosaic. The construction of the Lachine Canal in 1825 was a catalyst for industrial growth, facilitating the movement of goods and bolstering Montreal's status as a commercial hub.

Quebec City, while less industrialized than Montreal, retained its role as a political and cultural center. The city's distinctive blend of French and British influences is evident in its architecture, cuisine, and traditions. The preservation of the Old Quebec district, with its narrow cobblestone streets and historic buildings, earned it a UNESCO World Heritage designation in 1985, underscoring its historical and cultural significance.

The 20th century ushered in profound changes for both cities. Montreal became a vibrant center for arts and culture, hosting international events like Expo 67 and the 1976 Summer

Olympics. The Quiet Revolution of the 1960s, a period of rapid social and political change in Quebec, saw a reawakening of French-Canadian identity and a push for greater autonomy within Canada. This era also marked a shift in the province's economic and political power, with Montreal playing a central role in the movement.

Quebec City, meanwhile, continued to serve as a bastion of French-Canadian culture and political thought. The city played a key role in the sovereignty movement, advocating for Quebec's independence from Canada. This period of political activism was characterized by intense debate and negotiation, culminating in referendums on Quebec's status within Canada.

Today, Montreal and Quebec City stand as vibrant testaments to their storied pasts. Their histories are not mere chronicles of events but living narratives that continue to shape their identities. The cities are celebrated for their unique blend of old-world charm and modern dynamism, offering visitors a rich tapestry of cultural experiences.

Montreal, with its cosmopolitan flair, is a city of neighborhoods, each with its own character and charm. From the historic streets of Old Montreal to the bohemian vibes of the Plateau, the city's diversity is its strength. Quebec City, with its well-preserved heritage and picturesque setting, offers a window into the past, inviting exploration and discovery.

Both cities are proud stewards of French-Canadian culture, their histories etched into the fabric of their streets, buildings, and communities. As they continue to evolve, Montreal and Quebec City remain beacons of cultural richness, inviting visitors to delve into their captivating histories and vibrant present.

How to Use This Travel Guide

Navigating the enchanting landscapes of Montreal and Quebec City through this travel guide can transform your journey into an enriching adventure. With a thoughtful approach, you'll uncover hidden gems, savor local culinary delights, and immerse yourself in the vibrant culture of these French-Canadian cities. This guide is designed to enhance your travel experience, providing everything you need to make the most of your visit.

Begin by familiarizing yourself with the structure of this guide. Each chapter is crafted to offer specific insights into various aspects of your trip, from planning and logistics to exploring cultural landmarks and enjoying local festivities. The chapters are organized in a logical sequence to help you seamlessly plan your itinerary, whether you're embarking on a short getaway or an extended exploration.

Start with the planning essentials. Before diving into the sights and experiences, acquaint yourself with the practical aspects of travel. Understand the regional climate and best times to visit, as the seasons can dramatically alter the landscape and activities available. This knowledge will help you pack appropriately and prepare for weather conditions, ensuring comfort and convenience throughout your stay.

Budgeting is a crucial step in planning your trip. This guide provides a realistic overview of what to expect in terms of expenses, from accommodation and dining to transportation and entertainment. By setting a budget early on, you can prioritize experiences that matter most to you, whether it's indulging in gourmet meals or participating in unique local events. Consider utilizing public transport systems, as both cities boast efficient networks that can save you money while offering a chance to experience the daily rhythm of life like a local.

Familiarize yourself with travel documents and health considerations. Ensure you have all necessary identification and travel permits, and check for any health advisories or vaccinations required. Safety tips included in this guide will help you navigate unfamiliar environments with confidence, allowing you to focus on the joy of exploration without undue concern.

When delving into the heart of Montreal and Quebec City, this guide serves as your compass to must-see landmarks and attractions. Detailed descriptions and historical context bring each site to life, enriching your understanding and appreciation. Whether you're marveling at the architectural grandeur of the Notre-Dame Basilica or strolling through the cobblestone streets of Old Quebec, you'll find background information that enhances your visit.

In addition to popular landmarks, this guide uncovers lesser-known treasures that offer a more intimate glimpse into local life. Venture beyond the beaten path to discover neighborhoods brimming with character, unique shops, and hidden cafes. These sections encourage exploration and spontaneity, inviting you to see the cities through the eyes of a local.

Cultural events and festivals are integral to the fabric of these cities, and this guide highlights key happenings throughout the year. Align your travel dates with these vibrant celebrations to experience the cities at their liveliest. From the pulsating rhythms of the Montreal Jazz Festival to the winter wonderland of Quebec's Winter Carnival, these events offer unforgettable memories and a deeper connection to the local culture.

For those seeking culinary adventures, the guide provides insights into local cuisine, offering recommendations for dining experiences that range from traditional to avant-garde. Savor iconic dishes and regional specialties, and consider visiting local markets to sample fresh produce and artisanal products. This culinary journey is a feast for the senses, offering flavors that embody the essence of French-Canadian culture.

Day trips are an excellent way to expand your itinerary beyond the city limits, and this guide outlines several enticing options. Explore the natural beauty of the surrounding regions, from the Laurentian Mountains to the scenic Île d'Orléans. Each destination is carefully chosen for its unique offerings, whether it's outdoor adventures, historical sites, or charming villages. Detailed itineraries and travel tips help you make the most of these excursions, ensuring a seamless and enjoyable experience.

Understanding local etiquette and language nuances is key to fostering positive interactions during your travels. This guide offers language tips and cultural insights to help you communicate effectively and respectfully. Whether you're ordering a meal, asking for directions, or engaging in conversation, these tools will enhance your interactions and build connections with locals.

As you navigate this guide, remember that flexibility and openness to new experiences are your greatest allies. Use the information provided as a foundation upon which to build your unique adventure. Embrace the unexpected and allow yourself to be guided by curiosity, as some of the most memorable travel moments come from unplanned discoveries.

To make the most of this guide, consider keeping a travel journal to document your experiences. Reflecting on your journey not only preserves memories but also deepens your appreciation for the places you've visited and the people you've met. Capture the sights, sounds, and emotions of your adventure, creating a personal narrative that you can revisit long after your trip has ended.

This travel guide is more than just a compilation of facts and recommendations; it's an invitation to explore, connect, and immerse yourself in the rich tapestry of Montreal and Quebec City. By using this guide thoughtfully, you embark on a journey that transcends sightseeing, inviting you to engage with the culture, history, and spirit of these remarkable cities.

Best Times to Visit

Choosing the best time to visit Montreal and Quebec City can significantly enhance your travel experience, allowing you to enjoy the unique offerings of each season. These cities, nestled in the heart of French Canada, experience distinct seasonal changes that each bring their own charm and activities. Understanding the climate and cultural events throughout the year will help you tailor your visit to match your interests and expectations.

Winter in Montreal and Quebec City, spanning from December to February, transforms the cities into a picturesque winter wonderland. Snow blankets the streets, creating a magical ambiance that is perfect for winter enthusiasts. Despite the chilly temperatures, often dropping well below freezing, this season is celebrated with fervor. Quebec City's Winter Carnival, one of the largest winter festivals in the world, draws visitors with its vibrant parades, ice sculptures, and outdoor activities. Montreal, too, embraces the cold with events like Igloofest, an outdoor electronic music festival held on the city's Old Port, where revelers dance the night away in sub-zero temperatures.

For those who relish winter sports, the surrounding areas offer numerous opportunities for skiing, snowboarding, and ice skating. The nearby Laurentian Mountains and Mont-Tremblant provide world-class ski resorts, perfect for a day trip to enjoy the slopes. In the cities, outdoor rinks, such as the iconic one in Old Montreal, invite visitors to glide across the ice while taking in the historic surroundings.

Spring, from March to May, heralds the awakening of nature and a gradual warming of temperatures. As the snow melts, the cities come alive with a renewed energy. Trees begin to bud, and flowers bloom, adding vibrant colors to the urban landscape. This is a wonderful time to explore the cities' parks and gardens, such as Montreal's Botanical Garden, which hosts a stunning display of flora from around the world.

Spring also marks the beginning of the festival season. Montreal's International Jazz Festival and Quebec City's Film Festival are just a few of the cultural highlights that attract artists and audiences. These events offer an excellent opportunity to experience the cities' thriving arts scenes and witness performances by world-renowned musicians and filmmakers.

Summer, lasting from June to August, is arguably the most popular time to visit. The warm weather invites locals and tourists alike to enjoy outdoor activities and festivals. Streets and parks are bustling with life, and the cities' terraces and patios are filled with people savoring the sunshine. The Montreal International Jazz Festival, the largest of its kind, draws hundreds of thousands of music lovers, offering an eclectic mix of performances across various venues.

During the summer, both cities host a plethora of events celebrating their rich cultural heritage. In Quebec City, the Festival d'été de Québec brings diverse musical acts to the city, creating an electric atmosphere. Meanwhile, Montreal's Just for Laughs Festival showcases comedic talent from around the globe, turning the city into a hub of laughter and entertainment.

Outdoor enthusiasts will find plenty to do in the summer months. The nearby Montmorency Falls, just outside Quebec City, offer hiking trails and breathtaking views, while the Lachine Canal in Montreal provides a picturesque setting for kayaking and cycling. Exploring these natural wonders allows visitors to appreciate the stunning landscapes that surround the urban centers.

Autumn, from September to November, is a season of transformation and tranquility. As the leaves change color, the cities are bathed in hues of red, orange, and gold. This is the perfect time for leisurely strolls through the historic districts of Old Montreal and Old Quebec, where the cobblestone streets and charming architecture are beautifully complemented by the fall foliage.

Autumn is also harvest season, and the region's culinary scene reflects this abundance. Local markets, such as Montreal's Jean-Talon Market, offer a bounty of fresh produce and artisanal goods. Food festivals and events celebrate the rich flavors of the season, inviting visitors to indulge in gourmet delights.

For those who appreciate a quieter atmosphere, autumn provides a more relaxed pace of life. The summer crowds have dwindled, and the cities offer a more intimate experience. This is an ideal time to visit museums and galleries, explore the cities' rich histories, and enjoy leisurely meals at some of the finest restaurants.

Ultimately, the best time to visit Montreal and Quebec City depends on your personal preferences and interests. Each season offers its own unique attractions and experiences, from the vibrant energy of summer festivals to the serene beauty of autumn landscapes. By considering what activities and events align with your interests, you can plan a visit that captures the essence of these captivating cities.

CHAPTER 1: PLANNING YOUR TRIP

Setting Your Budget: What to Expect

Embarking on a journey to Montreal and Quebec City promises a rich tapestry of experiences, but setting a budget is crucial for ensuring that your adventures align with your financial expectations. Understanding the costs associated with accommodation, dining, transportation, and activities will allow you to maximize your experience without encountering financial surprises. With a well-planned budget, you can focus on savoring the vibrant culture and history these cities have to offer.

Accommodation is often the largest expense in any travel budget, and the options in Montreal and Quebec City range from luxurious hotels to budget-friendly hostels. In Montreal, the downtown area and the historic district of Old Montreal offer a variety of accommodations, with prices varying significantly based on location and amenities. In Quebec City, staying within or near Old Quebec provides a charming experience, though it may be more expensive than accommodations further afield. Consider booking in advance to take advantage of early-bird discounts and explore alternative lodging options such as vacation rentals or bed-and-breakfasts for a more personalized experience.

Dining in these cities is a culinary adventure, with opportunities to indulge in both high-end gourmet dining and affordable local delights. Montreal is famous for its diverse food scene, offering everything from trendy eateries to classic delis serving the city's renowned smoked meat sandwiches. Quebec City boasts a rich culinary heritage, with many restaurants offering traditional French-Canadian fare. To manage your dining budget, mix fine dining with visits to local markets and food stalls, where you can enjoy delicious meals at a fraction of the cost. Sampling street food and indulging in casual bistros will allow you to experience the local cuisine without overspending.

Transportation costs can vary depending on your chosen mode of travel. Both cities have efficient public transport systems, including buses and metro lines, which offer affordable and convenient ways to navigate urban areas. Consider purchasing daily or weekly passes if you plan to use public transport frequently. Car rentals are another option, especially if you intend to explore the surrounding regions. However, parking in the city can be costly, so weigh the convenience against potential expenses. For a more leisurely experience, walking or cycling can be enjoyable and budget-friendly ways to explore the cities' neighborhoods.

Activities and attractions are essential components of your travel experience, and planning these expenses in advance will help you stay within budget. Both cities offer a wealth of free or low-cost attractions, such as parks, historic sites, and public art installations. In Montreal, the Mount Royal Park provides stunning views and outdoor activities at no cost, while Quebec City's Dufferin Terrace offers breathtaking vistas of the St. Lawrence River. Museums and galleries often have discounted admission days or special offers, so check their schedules and plan your visits accordingly. Allocate a portion of your budget for must-see attractions and prioritize experiences that resonate most with your interests.

Shopping for souvenirs and mementos is a delightful part of any trip, but it's important to set limits to avoid overspending. Focus on unique, locally-made items that capture the essence of your visit, such as artisanal crafts, local delicacies, or regional wines. By purchasing thoughtfully, you can bring home meaningful keepsakes without straining your budget.

Travel insurance is an often-overlooked expense that can provide peace of mind during your trip. While it adds to your upfront costs, insurance can save you from unforeseen expenses related to medical emergencies, trip cancellations, or lost luggage. Research different policies and choose one that offers comprehensive coverage at a reasonable price.

Consider currency exchange rates and fees when planning your budget, as fluctuations can impact your spending power. Using credit cards with no foreign transaction fees can be advantageous, but having some local currency on hand for small purchases and tips is also wise. Exchange money at reputable institutions or withdraw from ATMs to get favorable rates.

To stretch your budget further, seek out discounts and deals offered by tourist offices or online platforms. City passes, which bundle admission to multiple attractions, can provide significant savings if you plan to visit several sites. Additionally, taking advantage of free walking tours or community events can enrich your experience without adding to your expenses.

Building a contingency fund into your budget is a prudent strategy, allowing for unexpected costs or spontaneous opportunities. This financial cushion ensures that you can adapt to changes or indulge in an unplanned activity without stress.

In summary, setting a realistic and flexible budget for your journey to Montreal and Quebec City is essential for a fulfilling travel experience. By considering accommodation, dining, transportation, activities, and other expenses, you can create a financial plan that supports your adventure while leaving room for spontaneity and discovery. With careful planning and mindful spending, you'll be well-equipped to enjoy the myriad of cultural and historical offerings these captivating cities have to offer.

Travel Documents, Health, and Safety

When preparing for a journey to Montreal and Quebec City, ensuring that you have the necessary travel documents, health precautions, and safety measures in place is paramount. These steps will not only facilitate a seamless travel experience but also provide peace of mind, allowing you to fully immerse yourself in the cultural richness these cities have to offer.

The first crucial aspect of your travel preparation involves ensuring you possess the appropriate travel documents. For international travelers, a valid passport is essential for entry into Canada. It's advisable to check the expiration date well in advance of your trip, as many countries require your passport to be valid for at least six months beyond your intended departure date. Depending on your nationality, you may also need a visa or an Electronic Travel Authorization (eTA) to enter Canada. It's wise to verify these requirements with the nearest Canadian consulate or embassy and apply for any necessary permits in advance to avoid last-minute complications.

In addition to entry documents, consider carrying photocopies of your passport and other important identification, such as a driver's license or national ID card. These copies can be invaluable in the event of loss or theft, making it easier to obtain replacements or navigate administrative processes. Store the originals and copies separately to minimize risk.

Health considerations are equally important when traveling. Before embarking on your journey, check if any vaccinations are required or recommended for travel to Canada. While there are generally no mandatory vaccines for entry, it's prudent to be up-to-date on routine immunizations such as measles, mumps, and rubella (MMR), as well as influenza, particularly if traveling during flu season.

Travel insurance is a vital component of your health preparations. Although Canada boasts an excellent healthcare system, medical services for non-residents can be costly. Comprehensive travel insurance should cover medical emergencies, hospital stays, and evacuation if necessary. Reading the fine print of your policy is crucial to ensure it covers the activities you plan to engage in, especially if they involve higher-risk sports or outdoor adventures.

Understanding the local healthcare system and knowing the locations of nearby hospitals or clinics can also be beneficial. Both Montreal and Quebec City have world-class medical facilities, so familiarize yourself with these resources and keep contact information handy during your stay.

Safety is another critical aspect of travel planning, and both cities are generally considered safe for visitors. However, practicing common-sense precautions can prevent mishaps. Be mindful of your surroundings, particularly in crowded tourist areas where pickpocketing can occur. Using a money belt or keeping valuables secured in an inside pocket can deter theft. In addition, avoid displaying large amounts of cash or expensive jewelry, as this can attract unwanted attention.

When exploring the cities, especially at night, stick to well-lit, populated areas and travel in groups if possible. Public transportation systems in both cities are reliable and secure, but it's always wise to remain vigilant, especially on late-night trips. Familiarize yourself with local emergency numbers and procedures, so you're prepared in the event of an unexpected situation.

Cultural awareness and respect for local customs can also enhance your safety and overall experience. French is the predominant language in both cities, particularly in Quebec City, and while many locals speak English, learning a few basic French phrases can go a long way in fostering goodwill and easing communication. Understanding cultural norms, such as tipping practices or appropriate dress codes for certain venues, will help you navigate social interactions smoothly.

In terms of transportation safety, if you plan to drive, ensure you have an international driving permit if required, and familiarize yourself with Canadian road rules and regulations. Winter driving in this region can be challenging, with icy roads and snowstorms, so if visiting during this season, ensure your vehicle is equipped with snow tires and emergency supplies. Alternatively, consider using public transportation or taxis to avoid the challenges of winter driving.

Environmental awareness is another important consideration, as Canada is known for its stunning natural landscapes. If your travel plans include outdoor activities, be prepared for varying weather conditions and respect nature by adhering to local guidelines and regulations. Carry appropriate gear for hiking or exploring, and always let someone know your itinerary if venturing into remote areas.

Lastly, staying informed about current events and advisories can enhance your travel safety. Monitor news sources and government travel advisories for any updates or alerts that may affect your plans. Registering with your embassy or consulate upon arrival can provide an additional layer of security, as they can offer assistance in emergencies or natural disasters.

By paying careful attention to travel documents, health precautions, and safety measures, you lay the groundwork for a smooth and enjoyable journey to Montreal and Quebec City. These preparations enable you to focus on the cultural, historical, and culinary delights that await, ensuring a memorable and worry-free travel experience.

Navigating the Cities: Public Transport and Car Rentals

Traveling through Montreal and Quebec City offers a fascinating blend of historic charm and modern vibrancy, making efficient navigation a key factor in maximizing your experience. Whether you're drawn to the bustling streets of Montreal or the quaint cobblestones of Old Quebec, understanding your transportation options will greatly enhance your visit. From public transit to car rentals, each mode of travel offers unique advantages depending on your itinerary and preferences.

Public transportation in these cities is a convenient and cost-effective way to explore urban areas. Montreal boasts an extensive public transit system, operated by the Société de transport de Montréal (STM), which includes a network of buses and a highly efficient metro system. The metro, with its four lines and 68 stations, is particularly useful for reaching key attractions and neighborhoods. Its underground routes are not only practical during the winter months but also provide a glimpse into Montreal's vibrant public art scene, with many stations featuring unique artworks.

When using the metro, consider purchasing an OPUS card, a reloadable smart card that provides easy access to buses and metro services. The card offers various fare options, including daily and weekly passes, which are ideal for visitors planning to use public transport frequently. The STM website and mobile app are excellent resources for planning your journeys, providing real-time updates and route information.

In Quebec City, the Réseau de transport de la Capitale (RTC) operates the public bus system. While Quebec City does not have a metro, the buses are reliable and cover most major areas, including popular tourist destinations. The Ecolobus, a small electric bus, is a convenient option for navigating the narrow streets of Old Quebec. Like Montreal, Quebec City offers fare cards and passes that can simplify your travel and potentially save money over single-trip tickets.

While public transport is efficient, there may be occasions when renting a car becomes advantageous, particularly for exploring regions outside the city centers. Car rentals offer flexibility, allowing you to tailor your itinerary without being bound by transit schedules. This is particularly useful if you plan to visit attractions like Mont-Tremblant or the charming villages along the Route des Navigateurs, where public transport options are limited.

Before renting a car, familiarize yourself with local driving regulations. In Canada, you drive on the right side of the road, and seat belts are mandatory for all passengers. If you're visiting in winter, ensure your rental vehicle is equipped with snow tires, as they are required by law in Quebec from December to March. Many rental agencies automatically include them, but it's wise to confirm this when booking.

Parking in Montreal and Quebec City can be challenging, especially in the city centers where spaces are limited and fees are high. Montreal offers several public parking lots and garages, as well as on-street parking with pay stations. Quebec City, known for its historic districts, has fewer parking options, making it advantageous to park outside the core and use public transport or walk. Be mindful of parking signs and regulations to avoid fines, and consider using parking apps to locate available spaces and compare prices.

Cycling is another popular mode of transport in both cities, offering an eco-friendly and enjoyable way to explore urban areas. Montreal, in particular, is renowned for its extensive network of bike paths, including the scenic Lachine Canal and the Route Verte, which connects various parts of the city. The BIXI bike-sharing system provides a convenient way to rent bikes for short trips, with numerous stations located throughout the city.

Quebec City also promotes cycling, with dedicated bike routes and rental services available. However, the city's hilly terrain can be challenging for some cyclists, so choose routes that match your comfort level and fitness. Cycling maps and resources can help you plan routes that highlight the cities' natural beauty and historic sites.

For those who prefer a more guided experience, consider using ride-sharing services or taxis, which are widely available in both cities. Ride-sharing apps offer the convenience of cashless transactions and the ability to track your route in real-time. Taxis can be hailed on the street or booked in advance, offering a reliable option for late-night travel or when public transport is less frequent.

Finally, walking remains one of the best ways to experience the charm and character of Montreal and Quebec City. Both cities are pedestrian-friendly, with many attractions, restaurants, and shops within walking distance of each other. Strolling through the cobblestone streets of Old Quebec or the vibrant neighborhoods of Montreal allows you to discover hidden gems and immerse yourself in the local atmosphere.

Choosing the right mode of transportation depends on your personal preferences, budget, and itinerary. By combining different options, you can create a seamless travel experience that caters to your interests and maximizes your time in these captivating cities. Whether you're navigating bustling city avenues or venturing into picturesque landscapes, understanding your transport options ensures a journey that is both efficient and enriching.

Seasonal Packing Guide

Packing strategically for a trip to Montreal and Quebec City is essential to ensure comfort and preparedness, regardless of the time of year. These cities experience a wide range of weather conditions, from the icy depths of winter to the humid warmth of summer. Understanding the seasonal variations and preparing accordingly will allow you to fully enjoy your journey without the worry of being caught off guard by unexpected weather changes.

Winter in Montreal and Quebec City, spanning December through February, is characterized by cold temperatures and significant snowfall. Packing for this season requires thoughtful layering to maintain warmth while allowing flexibility for indoor and outdoor activities. Start with a base layer of thermal or moisture-wicking fabric to keep your body dry. Add a middle layer for insulation, such as a fleece or wool sweater, which will trap heat. Your outer layer should be a waterproof and wind-resistant coat, preferably insulated, to protect against snow and wind chill.

Accessories are crucial during winter months. A warm hat, scarf, and gloves are indispensable for protecting extremities from the cold. Opt for insulated and waterproof footwear to navigate snowy and icy streets with ease, and consider adding thermal socks for extra warmth. Ice cleats or traction aids can be beneficial if you plan to explore less-trafficked areas where walkways might be slippery.

Spring, from March to May, brings a gradual transition to milder weather, but it can still be unpredictable. Packing layers is key, as temperatures can vary widely throughout the day. A lightweight jacket or raincoat is advisable, as spring showers are common. Including an umbrella and waterproof footwear in your luggage will keep you dry during unexpected downpours. As temperatures warm, you can shed layers and enjoy the blossoming parks and gardens without discomfort.

Summer, which spans June to August, is warm and humid, making lightweight, breathable clothing essential. Pack cotton or linen fabrics to stay cool, and include a wide-brimmed hat and sunglasses for sun protection. Sunscreen is a must for safeguarding your skin during outdoor activities. Comfortable walking shoes or sandals are recommended for exploring the cities on foot, as summer often involves a lot of strolling between attractions and festivals.

For evening outings, consider packing a light sweater or jacket, as temperatures can dip after sunset. Summer is also festival season, so you may want to include a versatile outfit suitable for both daytime activities and nighttime events, allowing you to transition seamlessly between casual and more formal settings.

Autumn, from September to November, is a time of transformation and vibrant foliage, with temperatures gradually cooling. Layers remain your best friend during this season, as mornings and evenings can be brisk while afternoons are often pleasantly warm. A medium-weight jacket, paired with long-sleeve shirts or sweaters, will keep you comfortable as you explore the crisp, colorful landscapes.

Packing a travel umbrella is advisable, as autumn can bring unexpected rain showers. Sturdy, waterproof shoes or boots are ideal for navigating leaf-covered paths or damp streets. This season also invites cozy accessories like scarves, which add warmth and style to your outfits without taking up much space in your luggage.

Regardless of the season, there are a few essential items that should always find a place in your suitcase when traveling to Montreal and Quebec City. A reusable water bottle is practical for staying hydrated while exploring. A small backpack or daypack will hold your essentials, such as maps, snacks, and a camera, allowing you to move freely without being encumbered by larger bags.

A universal power adapter is necessary for international travelers, ensuring that your devices remain charged and ready for use. If you plan to explore the outdoors, consider packing a small first-aid kit with band-aids, antiseptic wipes, and pain relievers for minor injuries or ailments.

For those who enjoy capturing memories, a camera or smartphone with a good camera is essential. The stunning architecture and picturesque landscapes of these cities offer countless photo opportunities. Bringing extra memory cards or a portable charger will ensure you're ready to capture every moment without interruption.

Lastly, consider the cultural context of your visit when packing. If you plan to visit religious sites or attend formal events, be sure to include clothing that respects local customs and dress codes. Researching specific venues in advance will help you select appropriate attire and avoid any potential discomfort or misunderstandings.

By packing thoughtfully for the seasons, you can focus on the rich experiences that Montreal and Quebec City offer, whether it be wandering through historic streets, enjoying local cuisine, or participating in vibrant festivals. Preparing for the weather and activities ensures a comfortable and enjoyable journey, allowing you to create lasting memories in these captivating destinations.

Understanding Local Etiquette and Language Tips

Navigating the cultural landscape of Montreal and Quebec City involves more than just visiting landmarks and indulging in local cuisine; it requires an understanding of the local etiquette and language nuances that define these vibrant communities. As the heart of French Canada, Quebec offers a unique blend of European charm and North American dynamism, with language and social customs playing a pivotal role in shaping interactions. Being mindful of these elements not only enriches your experience but also fosters a deeper connection with the locals.

French is the official language of Quebec, and while many residents in Montreal are bilingual, speaking both French and English, Quebec City tends to have a higher proportion of French speakers. A fundamental language tip for travelers is to learn a few basic French phrases. Simple greetings like "Bonjour" (Hello) and "Merci" (Thank you) go a long way in showing respect and willingness to engage with the local culture. Attempting to speak French, even if it's just a few words, is often appreciated and can lead to more amicable interactions. For those not fluent in French, carrying a pocket phrasebook or using a language app can be extremely useful.

In social settings, greetings are important. The French custom of greeting with a kiss on each cheek, known as "la bise," is common among friends and acquaintances, though a handshake suffices in more formal or initial meetings. It's polite to wait for the other person to initiate the greeting style to avoid any awkwardness. Titles and forms of address are also significant; using "Monsieur" or "Madame" followed by the person's last name is respectful in formal situations.

Understanding local dining etiquette can enhance your culinary experiences. Meals in Quebec are often seen as a time to relax and enjoy, so rushing through a meal might be considered impolite. When dining out, it's customary to greet the restaurant staff upon entering and thank them upon leaving. Tipping is standard practice, with 15-20% of the total bill being the norm in restaurants and cafes. If you're invited to a local's home, bringing a small gift such as wine or chocolates is a thoughtful gesture.

Quebecers are known for their politeness and appreciation for courtesy. Saying "Excusez-moi" (Excuse me) when navigating crowded spaces or "S'il vous plaît" (Please) when making requests demonstrates good manners. Public displays of frustration or impatience are generally frowned upon, so maintaining a calm and respectful demeanor is advisable.

When using public transportation, it's polite to give up your seat for the elderly, pregnant women, or those with disabilities. Speaking quietly and keeping phone conversations brief is also appreciated, as it maintains a peaceful environment for everyone on board.

Quebec's rich cultural tapestry is celebrated through numerous festivals and events throughout the year. Participating in these can offer insight into local traditions and values. Whether it's enjoying the music at the Montreal International Jazz Festival or marveling at the ice sculptures during Quebec City's Winter Carnival, engaging with these events can deepen your understanding of the cultural fabric.

Respect for local customs extends to religious and historical sites. When visiting churches or historic landmarks, dressing modestly and refraining from loud conversations are signs of respect. Photography may be restricted in certain areas, so it's prudent to check guidelines and seek permission if unsure.

Environmental consciousness is also a valued aspect of life in Quebec. Recycling and composting are widely practiced, and there is a strong emphasis on preserving natural spaces. Participating in these practices during your stay, such as disposing of waste in designated bins and minimizing plastic use, aligns with local values and contributes to sustainability efforts.

Quebecers are proud of their cultural heritage, and discussions about Quebecois identity, history, and politics can be passionate. While these topics can be fascinating, it's advisable to approach them with sensitivity and an open mind, as opinions may vary widely.

Finally, embracing the spirit of "La Joie de Vivre," or the joy of living, is perhaps the most fulfilling way to engage with Quebec's culture. This concept emphasizes savoring life's pleasures, whether through food, art, or nature. By immersing yourself in this way of life, you not only enrich your travel experience but also gain a deeper appreciation for the unique essence of Quebec.

Being mindful of language and etiquette as you navigate Montreal and Quebec City enhances your interactions and fosters a genuine connection with the people and places you encounter. This awareness not only opens doors to authentic experiences but also allows you to appreciate the rich cultural tapestry that defines this vibrant region.

CHAPTER 2: MUST-SEE LANDMARKS IN MONTREAL

Old Montreal: Exploring the Historic Heart

Old Montreal, the historic heart of the city, offers a captivating journey through time with its cobblestone streets, stunning architecture, and vibrant atmosphere. As one of North America's most well-preserved historic districts, Old Montreal invites visitors to step back into a bygone era while enjoying the modern amenities and attractions that make it a must-see destination.

Strolling through Old Montreal is akin to walking through a living museum, where each building and street tells a story. The area is rich with history, dating back to its founding in 1642. Begin your exploration at Place d'Armes, a bustling square surrounded by significant landmarks. The Notre-Dame Basilica, with its twin towers and ornate interior, dominates the square. This Gothic Revival masterpiece, completed in 1829, is renowned for its intricate woodwork, vibrant stained glass, and a magnificent pipe organ. Attending a light and sound show inside the basilica offers a mesmerizing way to appreciate its beauty and history.

Adjacent to Place d'Armes is the Old Seminary of Saint-Sulpice, one of Montreal's oldest buildings. Constructed in 1684, its simplicity contrasts with the grandeur of the basilica, yet it holds its own charm with a peaceful garden hidden behind its stone walls. The seminary's historic significance and architectural elegance make it a worthwhile stop on any itinerary.

As you make your way through the narrow streets, you'll encounter the Pointe-à-Callière Museum, Montreal's archaeology and history complex. Built atop the city's birthplace, this museum provides a fascinating insight into Montreal's past through interactive exhibits and archaeological sites. Descending into the museum's underground levels reveals remnants of the city's original structures, offering a tangible connection to the early settlers who shaped Montreal.

A short walk from the museum leads to the Old Port, a lively waterfront area that serves as both a historical site and a hub for contemporary entertainment. Here, you can enjoy a scenic stroll along the St. Lawrence River, take a ride on the Montreal Observation Wheel for panoramic views of the city, or relax at the Clock Tower Beach. The Old Port is also home to seasonal events and festivals, providing a dynamic backdrop to your visit.

Venture further into Old Montreal, and you'll discover Rue Saint-Paul, the oldest street in the city. This charming thoroughfare is lined with boutiques, galleries, cafes, and restaurants, each housed in historic buildings that exude character. Whether you're interested in shopping for unique souvenirs, savoring a meal at a local bistro, or simply soaking up the ambiance, Rue Saint-Paul offers a delightful experience.

For art enthusiasts, the Bonsecours Market is a must-visit. This iconic domed building, once a public market, now houses artisan shops and galleries showcasing Quebecois talent. The market's grand architecture and diverse offerings make it a cultural treasure within Old Montreal.

Nearby, the Notre-Dame-de-Bon-Secours Chapel, often referred to as the Sailors' Church, stands as a beacon of history and spirituality. Dating back to 1771, the chapel features maritime-themed artifacts and beautiful stained glass windows. Climbing to the chapel's rooftop rewards visitors with stunning views of the city and the river.

As you explore, take the time to enjoy the culinary delights that Old Montreal has to offer. The district is home to a variety of dining options, from cozy cafes to gourmet restaurants. Indulge in traditional Quebecois dishes, such as poutine or tourtière, or savor French-inspired cuisine that reflects Montreal's European heritage. Many establishments offer outdoor seating, allowing you to dine al fresco and soak in the unique atmosphere.

Old Montreal is also a vibrant nightlife destination, with numerous bars and pubs offering live music and entertainment. The area's nightlife scene caters to diverse tastes, whether you're in the mood for a relaxed evening with friends or a lively night out.

For those interested in delving deeper into the district's history, guided tours are available, offering insights into the stories and legends that have shaped Old Montreal. Walking tours, led by knowledgeable guides, provide an engaging way to learn about the area's rich heritage and architectural marvels.

The charm of Old Montreal lies in its ability to seamlessly blend the past with the present. As you wander through its historic streets, you'll encounter a city that embraces its heritage while celebrating its dynamic cultural scene. Each corner reveals a new facet of Old Montreal's identity, inviting you to explore, discover, and connect with a city that continues to captivate visitors from around the world.

Whether you're drawn to Old Montreal for its history, its architecture, or its vibrant atmosphere, your exploration of this district will undoubtedly leave a lasting impression. The blend of old-world charm and modern vitality creates an unforgettable experience, making Old Montreal a highlight of any visit to the city.

Notre-Dame Basilica: A Masterpiece of Gothic Revival

Notre-Dame Basilica stands as a testament to Montreal's rich history and architectural grandeur. Nestled in the heart of Old Montreal, this iconic edifice is not just a place of worship; it's a masterpiece of Gothic Revival architecture, drawing visitors from around the globe to admire its beauty and intricate design.

The basilica's story begins in the early 19th century, a period of expansion and transformation for the city. As Montreal grew, so did the need for a larger place of worship to accommodate its burgeoning Catholic population. In 1823, the decision was made to construct a new church that would reflect the city's aspirations and serve as a spiritual and cultural beacon. The task of designing this monumental structure fell to James O'Donnell, an Irish-American architect renowned for his expertise in Gothic Revival architecture.

O'Donnell's vision for the basilica was ambitious. He envisioned a grand structure that would echo the great cathedrals of Europe while incorporating elements unique to Montreal's identity. Construction began in 1824, and over the next five years, craftsmen and artisans dedicated themselves to bringing O'Donnell's vision to life. The basilica officially opened its doors in 1829, though its stunning interior would take several more decades to complete.

Stepping inside Notre-Dame Basilica is an awe-inspiring experience. Visitors are immediately struck by the vibrant hues and intricate details that adorn the interior. The church's vaulted ceilings reach skyward, creating a sense of space and grandeur that is both humbling and uplifting. The use of polychrome decoration, a hallmark of Gothic Revival architecture, infuses the space with color and light, enhancing the spiritual atmosphere.

One of the basilica's most striking features is its altar, a masterpiece of craftsmanship and artistry. Designed by the architect Victor Bourgeau in the latter half of the 19th century, the altar is a focal point of devotion and beauty. Intricately carved from wood and adorned with gold leaf, it depicts scenes from the life of the Virgin Mary, to whom the basilica is dedicated. The altar's grandeur is complemented by a series of stained glass windows that line the nave and choir, casting ethereal patterns of light and color throughout the space.

These stained glass windows are a marvel in their own right. Unlike many European cathedrals, which often depict biblical scenes, the windows of Notre-Dame Basilica tell the story of Montreal's religious history. They portray pivotal moments in the city's development, from the arrival of the first French missionaries to the founding of major religious institutions. This narrative approach not only enhances the basilica's spiritual ambiance but also connects visitors to the rich tapestry of Montreal's past.

The basilica is also home to a magnificent Casavant Frères pipe organ, installed in 1891. With over 7,000 pipes, this organ is not only an instrument of great power and range but also a work of art. Its sound fills the vast space with music that resonates deeply within the listener, enhancing the transcendent experience of visiting the basilica.

In addition to its architectural and artistic splendors, Notre-Dame Basilica holds a special place in the cultural life of Montreal. It has been the site of numerous significant events, from state funerals of prominent figures to celebrated concerts and performances. Its acoustics and ambiance make it a sought-after venue for musicians and performers, further cementing its status as a cultural landmark.

Visitors to the basilica may also have the opportunity to witness "AURA," a multimedia spectacle that presents the basilica in a new light. This immersive experience combines light, sound, and music to highlight the architectural beauty of the space, offering a unique perspective on the basilica's artistic and spiritual dimensions.

While the grandeur of Notre-Dame Basilica is undeniable, its true essence lies in its role as a living testament to faith, community, and history. It is a place where the sacred and the cultural intersect, offering solace and inspiration to all who enter its doors. Whether you are drawn by its architectural beauty, its rich history, or its spiritual significance, a visit to Notre-Dame Basilica promises to be a memorable and enriching experience.

As you stand beneath the soaring arches and gaze upon the intricate details, you become part of a continuum that stretches back nearly two centuries. The basilica's enduring presence speaks to the resilience and vision of those who built it, as well as the countless individuals who have found peace and inspiration within its walls. In Notre-Dame Basilica, the past and present converge, creating a space that transcends time and invites reflection and wonder.

Mount Royal Park: Hiking and Scenic Views

Mount Royal Park, a sprawling green oasis amid the bustling metropolis of Montreal, offers an idyllic escape for nature lovers and outdoor enthusiasts. Designed by the renowned landscape architect Frederick Law Olmsted, who also co-designed New York's Central Park, Mount Royal Park is a testament to natural beauty and thoughtful design. The park's trails and scenic vistas provide the perfect setting for hiking, picnicking, and enjoying breathtaking views of the city and beyond.

Ascending Mount Royal is an adventure that rewards hikers with a sense of escape from urban life without ever leaving the city. The mountain itself, a volcanic-related hill, is the centerpiece of the park and stands as one of Montreal's most iconic landmarks. At an elevation of 233 meters, it offers panoramic views that capture the essence of the city's skyline and the surrounding landscape. The park covers over 200 hectares, providing ample space to wander and explore.

The main trailhead begins at the George-Étienne Cartier Monument, a grand statue that serves as a popular gathering spot. From here, visitors can embark on the most traveled route to the summit—the Olmsted Trail. This wide, gravel path meanders through the park's lush forests and open meadows, making it accessible to hikers of all skill levels. The gradual incline allows for a leisurely ascent, encouraging hikers to savor the natural surroundings.

Along the way, the trail reveals hidden gems, including Beaver Lake, a serene spot perfect for a restful pause. In the warmer months, the lake becomes a haven for picnickers and paddle boaters, while in winter, it transforms into a picturesque skating rink. The changing seasons paint the park in different hues, offering a unique experience throughout the year.

As hikers continue their journey, they encounter a network of smaller trails that branch off from the main path. These trails invite exploration and lead to secluded areas where the forest's canopy provides a tranquil retreat. Birdwatchers will find delight in the diverse avian species that inhabit the park, while photographers can capture the play of light filtering through the trees.

Reaching the summit, known as the Kondiaronk Belvedere, hikers are greeted with an expansive terrace that offers one of the most stunning views of Montreal. Named after a Huron chief who played a significant role in the region's history, the belvedere provides a sweeping panorama of the city, the St. Lawrence River, and the distant Appalachian foothills. This vantage point is particularly captivating at sunrise or sunset, when the city is bathed in golden light.

Adjacent to the belvedere is the Mount Royal Chalet, a charming building with a rich history dating back to 1932. The chalet serves as a welcome resting place, offering refreshments and a glimpse into the park's past through interpretative displays. Its architecture, reminiscent of a grand lodge, adds to the ambiance of the summit experience.

For those seeking a more challenging hike, the park offers additional trails that wind through its varied terrain. The Summit Woods Trail provides a more rugged experience, leading hikers through densely forested areas and rewarding them with glimpses of wildlife. These trails allow for a more intimate connection with the natural environment and are perfect for those who wish to venture off the beaten path.

Beyond hiking, Mount Royal Park offers a plethora of activities that cater to different interests. Cyclists can enjoy dedicated paths that circle the mountain, providing a thrilling ride with scenic views. In winter, the park becomes a wonderland for snowshoeing and cross-country skiing, with trails maintained for these activities. Tobogganing down the park's slopes is a favorite pastime for families, adding an element of fun and excitement to the winter landscape.

Cultural and community events often take place in the park, drawing locals and visitors alike. Tam-Tams, a weekly drum circle held near the George-Étienne Cartier Monument, fills the air with rhythmic beats and creates a lively atmosphere. This spontaneous gathering of musicians and dancers is a beloved Montreal tradition that embodies the city's vibrant and inclusive spirit.

Preserving the ecological integrity of Mount Royal Park is a priority, and visitors are encouraged to respect the natural environment. Staying on designated trails, disposing of waste responsibly, and being mindful of wildlife are essential practices that ensure the park remains a pristine sanctuary for generations to come.

Whether you're seeking a peaceful retreat, an invigorating hike, or a chance to connect with Montreal's natural beauty, Mount Royal Park offers it all. The combination of accessible trails, stunning vistas, and diverse activities makes it a cherished destination for both locals and tourists. Each visit to Mount Royal Park promises new discoveries and moments of reflection, inviting all who come to experience the harmonious blend of nature and urban life.

The Montreal Museum of Fine Arts: Art Through the Ages

The Montreal Museum of Fine Arts stands as a beacon of culture and creativity, offering a comprehensive journey through the evolution of art across centuries. As one of the largest and most prestigious art museums in Canada, it houses an extensive collection that spans various periods, styles, and cultures, making it an essential destination for art enthusiasts and casual visitors alike.

Founded in 1860 by a group of prominent Montreal citizens, the museum has grown exponentially over the years. Today, it occupies multiple pavilions, each dedicated to different facets of its vast collection. The museum's architecture blends historic and modern elements, reflecting both its storied past and its commitment to contemporary innovation. As visitors approach the museum, they are greeted by the striking facade of the Michal and Renata Hornstein Pavilion, a landmark of neoclassical design that sets the tone for the rich artistic experience within.

Upon entering the museum, the journey begins with a collection of Canadian and Quebecois art. This section celebrates the country's diverse artistic heritage, featuring works from Indigenous artists, early European settlers, and contemporary creators. The Indigenous art collection is particularly noteworthy, showcasing traditional and modern pieces that highlight the rich cultural traditions and contemporary voices of First Nations, Inuit, and Métis artists. These works not only provide insight into the artistic practices of Indigenous peoples but also engage with broader themes of identity, resilience, and cultural preservation.

Moving through the museum, visitors encounter an impressive array of European art, spanning from the Renaissance to the modern era. The collection includes masterpieces by renowned artists such as Rembrandt, El Greco, and Monet, each piece offering a glimpse into the artistic movements and historical contexts of its time. The

Baroque and Rococo sections captivate with their opulence and dramatic flair, while the Impressionist gallery enchants with its vibrant colors and innovative techniques. These works invite viewers to explore the evolution of artistic expression, from the meticulous realism of the Renaissance to the bold experimentation of modern art.

The museum also boasts a significant collection of international art, encompassing works from Africa, Asia, the Middle East, and the Americas. This global perspective enriches the museum's offerings, providing a diverse array of artistic traditions and perspectives. The African collection features a range of traditional masks and sculptures, each piece imbued with cultural significance and artistic mastery. Meanwhile, the Asian art gallery presents delicately crafted ceramics, textiles, and paintings, reflecting the region's rich artistic heritage and influence.

In addition to its permanent collections, the Montreal Museum of Fine Arts is renowned for its dynamic temporary exhibitions. These exhibitions often focus on specific themes, artists, or periods, providing fresh insights and opportunities for discovery. Past exhibitions have explored topics as varied as the art of haute couture, the works of contemporary Indigenous artists, and the influence of music on visual art. These curated experiences offer visitors a chance to engage with art in new and unexpected ways, sparking curiosity and dialogue.

The museum's commitment to education and community engagement is evident in its wide range of programs and initiatives. Workshops, lectures, and guided tours are available for visitors of all ages, fostering a deeper understanding and appreciation of art. The museum's educational programs aim to make art accessible to everyone, encouraging creativity and critical thinking through hands-on experiences and interactive learning.

One of the museum's highlights is its state-of-the-art concert hall, the Bourgie Hall, which hosts a variety of musical performances throughout the year. This unique venue enhances the museum's cultural offerings by bridging the visual and performing arts. Concerts range from classical symphonies to contemporary ensembles, creating a rich tapestry of auditory and visual experiences that complement the museum's artistic mission.

Visitors can also enjoy the museum's beautifully landscaped sculpture garden, an outdoor space that invites reflection and exploration. This serene setting features contemporary sculptures by Canadian and international artists, offering a harmonious blend of art and nature. The garden serves as a peaceful retreat and a testament to the museum's dedication to integrating art into everyday life.

The Montreal Museum of Fine Arts is more than just a repository of art; it is a vibrant cultural hub that celebrates the power of creativity to inspire, challenge, and transform. Its diverse collections and innovative programs engage visitors in a dialogue with art that transcends time and place. Whether you are an avid art lover or a curious newcomer, the museum offers an enriching experience that leaves a lasting impression, inviting you to return and discover anew the ever-changing world of art.

Jean-Talon Market: A Taste of Local Life

Jean-Talon Market, nestled in the heart of Montreal's vibrant Little Italy, is a sensory feast that captures the essence of local life. As one of the largest public markets in North America, it serves as a bustling hub for food lovers, farmers, and artisans alike. Open year-round, the market beckons visitors with its colorful displays and enticing aromas, offering a genuine taste of Montreal's diverse culinary landscape.

Stepping into Jean-Talon Market is an immersion into a world where the lines between producer and consumer blur, fostering a sense of community and connection. Rows of stalls overflow with fresh produce, much of it sourced from Quebec's fertile farmlands. Juicy tomatoes, crisp apples, and vibrant berries catch the eye, their colors reflecting the changing seasons. Vendors proudly display their harvests, eager to share the stories behind their produce. Engaging with these local farmers provides insights into the region's agricultural practices and offers an opportunity to learn about the importance of supporting local economies.

The market is also a treasure trove for those seeking artisanal products. Cheese lovers can indulge in a wide array of Quebec's finest cheeses, from creamy bries to sharp cheddars. Many of these cheeses are crafted by artisanal producers who adhere to traditional methods, ensuring a quality that is both authentic and delectable. Sampling these cheeses is an experience in itself, each bite offering a unique flavor profile that reflects the terroir of the region.

Beyond produce and dairy, Jean-Talon Market celebrates the multicultural fabric of Montreal through its diverse culinary offerings. A stroll through the market reveals an array of international flavors, from Middle Eastern spices and Italian pastas to Vietnamese spring rolls and Caribbean jerk chicken. This global variety is a testament to Montreal's rich immigrant heritage, where diverse cultures coexist and contribute to the city's dynamic food scene.

For those looking to savor local specialties, the market offers an abundance of Quebecois delicacies. Maple syrup, a staple of Quebec's culinary identity, is available in various forms, from classic syrups to maple-infused candies and butters. Sampling these products provides a sweet introduction to one of the region's most beloved exports. Another must-try is tourtière, a savory meat pie that embodies the warmth and comfort of traditional Quebecois home cooking. Vendors often have their own variations of this classic dish, offering a range of flavors to suit different palates.

Jean-Talon Market is not just a place for shopping; it's a vibrant social space where locals and visitors mingle over shared culinary passions. The market's cafes and eateries provide perfect spots for relaxation and people-watching. Sipping a freshly brewed coffee or enjoying a pastry while observing the lively market scene is a quintessential Montreal experience. These moments of pause amid the market's energy offer a chance to appreciate the slower pace of life and the joy of simple pleasures.

For those interested in honing their culinary skills, the market hosts cooking demonstrations and workshops throughout the year. These events, often led by local chefs and food experts, provide valuable insights into cooking techniques and recipes that highlight seasonal ingredients. Participating in these workshops is an excellent way to deepen your understanding of Quebecois cuisine and gain practical skills to recreate these flavors at home.

Visiting Jean-Talon Market is also an opportunity to engage with sustainable practices. Many vendors prioritize organic and eco-friendly farming methods, contributing to a healthier environment and community. By choosing to support these vendors, visitors can make a positive impact on the local food system and contribute to a more sustainable future.

Exploring the market with a curious mind and open palate leads to unexpected discoveries. Whether it's stumbling upon a rare heirloom vegetable, tasting a handcrafted charcuterie, or chatting with a passionate vendor about their craft, Jean-Talon Market offers countless moments of delight. Each visit is a unique adventure, with something new to discover and savor.

Jean-Talon Market embodies the spirit of Montreal—a city that thrives on its diversity, creativity, and love for good food. It captures the essence of what makes Montreal a culinary capital: a commitment to quality, a celebration of multiculturalism, and a deep-rooted connection to the land and its bounty. For anyone seeking an authentic taste of local life, Jean-Talon Market is an essential stop, offering a rich tapestry of flavors and experiences that reflect the soul of the city.

Hidden Gems in the Plateau Mont-Royal Neighborhood

The Plateau Mont-Royal neighborhood, a vibrant and eclectic area of Montreal, is renowned for its bohemian charm and artistic spirit. While many are familiar with its bustling streets, trendy cafes, and colorful murals, the Plateau also harbors hidden gems that offer a deeper glimpse into the neighborhood's unique character. These lesser-known spots provide a rich tapestry of experiences, blending history, creativity, and community that define this beloved part of the city.

Begin your exploration with a visit to the Saint-Louis Square, a picturesque park tucked away amidst the urban landscape. This charming square, with its Victorian-era architecture and tranquil fountain, offers a serene escape for those seeking a moment of quiet reflection. The surrounding streets are lined with historic row houses, each boasting intricate wrought-iron balconies and colorful facades that evoke a sense of nostalgia. It's a perfect spot to enjoy a book, have a picnic, or simply watch the world go by.

Venture a little further, and you'll stumble upon the hidden alleyways that crisscross the Plateau. These narrow passages, adorned with vibrant street art, are a testament to Montreal's thriving creative scene. Local artists use these spaces as canvases to express their talents, creating ever-changing galleries that reflect the neighborhood's dynamic energy. Walking through these alleys offers a glimpse into the community's soul, where art and life intersect in unexpected and delightful ways.

For a taste of local culture, head to the lesser-known venues that host intimate performances and events. The Plateau is home to a variety of small theaters and music venues that showcase the talents of emerging artists. Places like La Sala Rossa and Casa del Popolo offer a cozy atmosphere where you can enjoy live music, poetry readings, and eclectic performances. These venues are often run by artists themselves, fostering a sense of community and collaboration that is integral to the Plateau's identity.

Food lovers will delight in the hidden culinary treasures scattered throughout the neighborhood. While the Plateau is famous for its bagels and poutine, it also boasts a diverse array of eateries that cater to every palate. Seek out the unassuming bistros and cafes tucked away on quiet side streets, where you can savor everything from authentic Middle Eastern cuisine to innovative vegan dishes. These establishments often use locally sourced ingredients, reflecting the neighborhood's commitment to sustainability and quality.

For those with a penchant for vintage and unique finds, the Plateau's thrift shops and boutiques are a treasure trove waiting to be explored. These independently owned stores offer an eclectic mix of clothing, accessories, and home decor, each piece with a story to tell. Whether you're hunting for a rare vinyl record, a quirky piece of art, or a retro fashion statement, the Plateau's shops are sure to surprise and delight.

The neighborhood's green spaces also offer hidden gems for those who know where to look. While Mount Royal Park is a popular destination, smaller parks like Parc La Fontaine provide a more intimate setting for enjoying nature. With its winding paths, serene pond, and lush greenery, Parc La Fontaine is a haven for outdoor enthusiasts and families alike. In the warmer months, it's common to see locals enjoying picnics, playing frisbee, or simply soaking up the sun.

Community gardens are another aspect of the Plateau that often goes unnoticed. These green oases, maintained by local residents, are scattered throughout the neighborhood and provide a space for urban gardening and community building. Visiting these gardens offers insight into the Plateau's strong sense of community and the residents' dedication to creating sustainable, shared spaces.

For a deeper understanding of the neighborhood's history, consider exploring some of the lesser-known historical sites. The Plateau has been home to various cultural communities over the years, each leaving its mark on the area. Walking tours led by local historians can reveal the stories behind the neighborhood's architecture and landmarks, offering a richer perspective on its past and present.

As the day winds down, head to one of the hidden rooftop terraces for a drink and a view of the city skyline. These secret spots are often found atop local bars and restaurants, providing a perfect vantage point to watch the sunset over the city. With a cocktail in hand and the cityscape stretching before you, it's easy to understand why the Plateau has captured the hearts of so many.

The Plateau Mont-Royal neighborhood's hidden gems are a testament to its vibrant and multifaceted nature. By venturing off the beaten path, you can discover the stories, people, and places that make the Plateau a living canvas of creativity and culture. Whether you're drawn to its artistic spirit, culinary delights, or community spaces, the Plateau invites you to explore and uncover the treasures that lie just beneath the surface.

The Historic Lachine Canal: Biking and Kayaking

The Historic Lachine Canal, a vital artery in Montreal's industrial past, has transformed into a vibrant leisure destination, offering a scenic escape for those seeking outdoor adventure. This 14.5-kilometer waterway, which once served as a crucial trade route bypassing the treacherous Lachine Rapids, now invites visitors to explore its picturesque settings by bike or kayak. It's a journey through time and nature, blending the city's rich history with the serene beauty of its waterfront.

Biking along the Lachine Canal is a popular activity, thanks to the well-maintained path that runs along its length. Cyclists of all levels can enjoy the flat, smooth trail, which offers a leisurely ride through some of Montreal's most charming neighborhoods. The path begins near the Old Port, where cobblestone streets and historic buildings set the stage for your journey. As you set off, the cityscape slowly gives way to more tranquil surroundings, with lush greenery and the gentle flow of the canal accompanying your ride.

The trail is dotted with points of interest that offer glimpses into the canal's storied past. Interpretive panels along the route provide context about the canal's construction in the early 19th century and its role in transforming Montreal into a major industrial hub. As you pedal, you can envision the bustling activity of the canal's heyday, when barges laden with goods navigated its waters, fueling the city's growth and prosperity.

One of the highlights of the cycling route is Atwater Market, a beloved Montreal institution. This bustling market, located just a short detour from the canal, is a perfect stop for refreshments. Here, you can sample local delicacies, from artisanal cheeses to freshly baked pastries, or pick up a picnic to enjoy by the water. The market's vibrant atmosphere offers a taste of local life and a chance to mingle with Montrealers going about their daily routines.

Continuing along the canal, you'll encounter the Saint-Henri neighborhood, an area steeped in history and culture. Once home to factories and workers' cottages, Saint-Henri has undergone a renaissance, evolving into a trendy district with cafes, galleries, and shops. The neighborhood's industrial past is still visible in its architecture, with many old buildings repurposed into creative spaces and lofts. This blend of old and new adds to the charm of the ride, offering a visual narrative of Montreal's resilience and adaptability.

As you near the end of the canal, the landscape becomes more expansive, with open skies and the distant silhouette of the Lachine Rapids. This section of the trail is less crowded, offering a peaceful retreat from the city's hustle and bustle. The canal widens here, creating a sense of space and tranquility that invites reflection and relaxation.

For those who prefer water-based exploration, kayaking on the Lachine Canal provides a unique perspective on its beauty. Renting a kayak is straightforward, with several outfitters located along the canal offering all the necessary equipment. Gliding on the water, kayakers can immerse themselves in the natural surroundings, experiencing the canal's gentle currents and the soothing sounds of nature.

Kayaking offers a closer connection to the canal's ecosystem, allowing you to observe wildlife up close. Ducks, herons, and other waterfowl are common sights, adding to the canal's serene ambiance. Paddling at your own pace, you can explore hidden coves and inlets, discovering quiet corners that are inaccessible by land. These secluded spots offer opportunities for solitude and contemplation, where the only sounds are the rhythmic dip of your paddle and the rustle of leaves in the breeze.

The Lachine Canal also hosts a variety of events and activities throughout the year, making it a lively destination for locals and visitors alike. Summer sees outdoor concerts, festivals, and community gatherings that transform the canal's banks into vibrant social spaces. Whether it's a pop-up art exhibit, a food truck festival, or a sunset yoga session, these events showcase the canal's role as a cultural hub and a place of connection.

Preserving the canal's historical and ecological integrity is a priority, and visitors are encouraged to respect the environment. Staying on designated paths, disposing of waste responsibly, and being mindful of wildlife contribute to the canal's sustainability and ensure it remains a cherished resource for future generations.

The Historic Lachine Canal is more than just a scenic route—it's a journey through Montreal's past and present, offering a blend of adventure, culture, and tranquility. Whether biking along its picturesque paths or kayaking its gentle waters, the canal invites you to explore and discover the stories that have shaped this iconic part of the city. With each turn of the pedal or stroke of the paddle, you become part of the canal's ongoing narrative, experiencing the harmony of nature and history in one of Montreal's most treasured settings.

Montreal's Underground City: An Urban Marvel

Beneath the vibrant streets of Montreal lies a hidden world, a sprawling network of tunnels and passageways known as the Underground City, or Réso. This urban marvel, extending for over 33 kilometers, is a testament to human ingenuity and the city's adaptability to its harsh climate. It offers a unique and fascinating way to navigate Montreal, particularly during the cold winter months when temperatures plummet and snow blankets the city.

The origins of the Underground City date back to the 1960s, when the first sections were constructed to connect major buildings and metro stations. What began as a practical solution to the challenges of winter commuting has since evolved into an extensive complex of interconnected shopping centers, hotels, office buildings, cultural venues, and more. Today, it is one of the largest underground complexes in the world, drawing both locals and tourists to its climate-controlled corridors.

Entering the Underground City is like stepping into a parallel universe where the hustle and bustle of the surface world continue, but with a unique twist. The subterranean landscape is a mix of sleek modern design and functional architecture, with clean lines, bright lighting, and open spaces that defy the usual claustrophobic expectations of underground environments. Signage is clear and abundant, guiding visitors through the maze of passages with ease.

One of the most compelling features of the Underground City is its seamless integration with Montreal's public transportation system. The network is anchored by several metro stations, including major hubs like Berri-UQAM and Bonaventure. This connectivity allows commuters to travel across the city without ever stepping outside, a convenience that is especially appreciated during inclement weather. For newcomers, mastering this system is a rite of passage, offering them a sense of belonging in this bustling metropolis.

Shopping is a major draw in the Underground City, with a vast array of retail options catering to all tastes and budgets. From high-end boutiques offering designer fashions to quirky shops selling local crafts, there's something for everyone. The Eaton Centre, Place Montreal Trust, and Complexe Desjardins are just a few of the shopping centers that form the backbone of this subterranean retail paradise. Shoppers can spend hours wandering from one complex to another, discovering new finds without ever having to brave the elements.

Dining options are equally diverse, with a range of eateries that reflect Montreal's multicultural culinary scene. Food courts offer quick and affordable meals, while sit-down restaurants provide more leisurely dining experiences. Whether you're in the mood for sushi, Italian, Middle Eastern, or traditional Quebecois fare, the Underground City has it all. It's the perfect place to take a break and refuel before continuing your exploration.

Beyond shopping and dining, the Underground City is home to a variety of cultural and entertainment venues. The Place des Arts, Montreal's premier performing arts complex, is accessible via the underground network, offering a convenient way to catch a concert, ballet, or theater performance. Art installations and exhibitions are also featured throughout the tunnels, adding a touch of creativity and inspiration to the daily commute.

The Underground City serves as a haven for those seeking refuge from Montreal's sometimes harsh climate. It's not uncommon to see joggers taking advantage of the climate-controlled environment for their daily runs, or families with strollers enjoying a leisurely stroll. The space is designed to accommodate a wide range of activities, making it a versatile and welcoming environment for all.

For those unfamiliar with the Underground City, navigating it can initially seem daunting. However, with a little patience and a sense of adventure, it soon becomes second nature. Maps are readily available, both online and in print, to help visitors plan their routes and discover new areas. Each section of the Underground City has its own character and attractions, offering endless opportunities for exploration.

The Underground City is more than just a network of tunnels; it's an integral part of Montreal's identity and a reflection of the city's resilience and creativity. It demonstrates how urban planning can adapt to environmental challenges and enhance the quality of life for its residents. As you wander through its corridors, you'll find yourself immersed in a world that is both familiar and entirely unique, a testament to the spirit of innovation that defines Montreal.

This subterranean marvel invites you to discover the hidden side of the city, where convenience meets culture and commerce meets creativity. Whether you're seeking refuge from the weather, indulging in retail therapy, or simply exploring out of curiosity, the Underground City offers a distinctive and captivating experience that is not to be missed.

CHAPTER 3: MUST-SEE LANDMARKS IN QUEBEC CITY

Old Quebec: A UNESCO World Heritage Site

Winding cobblestone streets, centuries-old architecture, and an air of old-world charm define Old Quebec, a UNESCO World Heritage Site that transports visitors back in time. Nestled within the heart of Quebec City, this historic district is a living museum, showcasing the rich tapestry of history and culture that has shaped the region since its founding in the early 17th century. As you step into Old Quebec, you are immediately enveloped by a sense of history and wonder, a place where stories of the past linger in every corner.

Old Quebec is divided into two distinct parts: Upper Town and Lower Town, each with its own unique character and attractions. Upper Town, perched on the cliffs overlooking the St. Lawrence River, is dominated by the iconic Château Frontenac, a grand hotel that has become synonymous with the city itself. This architectural masterpiece, with its turrets and copper roof, offers breathtaking views of the river and the surrounding landscape. It is a must-visit for anyone exploring Old Quebec, whether for a luxurious stay or simply to admire its grandeur.

A short walk from the Château takes you to the Dufferin Terrace, a wide boardwalk that stretches along the edge of the cliffs. Here, visitors can enjoy panoramic vistas of the river and the Laurentian Mountains beyond. The terrace is a popular spot for leisurely strolls, street performances, and people-watching. In winter, the Terrasse Dufferin Slides offer a thrilling tobogganing experience that delights both children and adults.

The streets of Upper Town are lined with historic buildings and landmarks, each with a story to tell. The Citadelle of Quebec, an active military installation, offers guided tours that delve into the city's military history and provide insight into its strategic importance. Nearby, the Notre-Dame de Québec Basilica-Cathedral, one of the oldest cathedrals in North America, invites visitors to admire its stunning architecture and spiritual ambiance.

As you descend to Lower Town, the atmosphere shifts to a lively and bustling scene. This area, known for its quaint boutiques, cafes, and art galleries, is a hub of activity. Place Royale, a charming square at the heart of Lower Town, is a focal point for visitors seeking to explore the city's colonial past. The square is home to the Notre-Dame-des-Victoires Church, a small yet significant place of worship that stands as a testament to the city's resilience and faith.

Lower Town's Petit-Champlain district, with its narrow streets and old-world charm, is reminiscent of a European village. Here, visitors can explore an array of artisanal shops, offering everything from handmade crafts to gourmet treats. The district is particularly enchanting during the winter months, when it is adorned with twinkling lights and festive decorations, creating a magical atmosphere that captivates the senses.

Old Quebec is not just a showcase of historical architecture; it is a vibrant community that celebrates its cultural heritage through festivals and events. One of the most famous is the

Winter Carnival, a lively celebration that embraces the joys of winter with parades, ice sculptures, and outdoor activities. This event draws visitors from around the world, eager to experience the unique charm of Quebec's winter wonderland.

For those interested in delving deeper into the history of Old Quebec, several museums offer rich insights into the city's past. The Musée de l'Amérique francophone explores the French influence in North America, while the Musée de la Civilisation provides a broader perspective on Quebec's cultural evolution. These institutions offer engaging exhibitions and interactive displays that bring history to life, making them essential stops for any history enthusiast.

Dining in Old Quebec is a culinary journey that reflects the region's rich heritage and diverse influences. From traditional Quebecois dishes to modern fusion cuisine, the area's restaurants offer a wide range of flavors to satisfy any palate. Local specialties such as poutine, tourtière, and maple-infused treats are must-tries for those seeking an authentic taste of Quebec. Many eateries are housed in historic buildings, adding an extra layer of charm to the dining experience.

Exploring Old Quebec is an invitation to step back in time and immerse yourself in the stories of the past. The district's well-preserved architecture and historical landmarks provide a glimpse into the lives of those who walked these streets centuries ago. Yet, Old Quebec is not frozen in time; it is a dynamic and evolving community that continues to celebrate its heritage while embracing modernity.

Whether wandering through its cobblestone streets, admiring its architectural wonders, or savoring its culinary delights, Old Quebec offers a rich and rewarding experience for all who visit. It is a place where history and culture intertwine, creating a tapestry of experiences that leave a lasting impression. As a UNESCO World Heritage Site, Old Quebec stands as a testament to the enduring legacy of its past, a place where the echoes of history continue to resonate in the present.

Château Frontenac: The Iconic Fairmont Hotel

Perched majestically atop Cap Diamant, overlooking the St. Lawrence River, Château Frontenac is more than just a hotel—it's an enduring symbol of Quebec City and a masterpiece of architectural grandeur. This iconic Fairmont hotel, with its distinctive green copper roof and castle-like silhouette, captures the imagination of visitors from around the world. As a living testament to the city's rich history and vibrant culture, Château Frontenac invites guests to step into a world of elegance, luxury, and storied past.

The history of Château Frontenac dates back to the late 19th century, when it was conceived as part of a series of grand railway hotels built by the Canadian Pacific Railway. Designed by American architect Bruce Price, the hotel was named after Louis de Buade, Count of Frontenac, a notable governor of New France. Since its opening in 1893, the Château has stood as a beacon of hospitality, hosting dignitaries, celebrities, and royalty within its opulent walls.

Walking through the grand entrance of Château Frontenac, guests are immediately enveloped in an atmosphere of timeless elegance. The hotel's interior is a blend of Victorian and French Renaissance styles, featuring intricate woodwork, stained glass windows, and lavish furnishings that evoke a sense of old-world charm. The lobby, with its soaring ceilings and grand chandeliers, sets the stage for a memorable stay, inviting guests to explore the history and luxury that define the Château experience.

Château Frontenac offers a range of accommodations, each designed to provide comfort and sophistication. The guest rooms and suites, many of which offer sweeping views of the St. Lawrence River or Old Quebec, are elegantly appointed with plush bedding, rich fabrics, and modern amenities. Each room is a sanctuary of relaxation, allowing guests to unwind in style while surrounded by the hotel's storied past.

Dining at Château Frontenac is a culinary journey that reflects Quebec's rich gastronomic heritage. The hotel's signature restaurant, Champlain, offers an exquisite menu of contemporary Quebecois cuisine, crafted with locally sourced ingredients and presented with artistic flair. Guests can savor dishes that celebrate the region's flavors, from succulent game meats to fresh seafood, all expertly paired with wines from the hotel's extensive cellar.

For a more casual dining experience, Bistro Le Sam provides a vibrant atmosphere where guests can enjoy a diverse menu of bistro classics and innovative cocktails. The bistro's terrace, overlooking the river, is a popular spot for al fresco dining in warmer months, offering a picturesque setting to enjoy a leisurely meal.

Château Frontenac also pays homage to its heritage with 1608 Wine and Cheese Bar, a sophisticated lounge where guests can indulge in a curated selection of fine wines and artisanal cheeses. The bar's elegant ambiance and stunning views make it an ideal spot for an evening of relaxation and indulgence.

Beyond its luxurious accommodations and dining, Château Frontenac offers a wealth of amenities and activities to enhance the guest experience. The hotel's spa provides a tranquil retreat, offering a range of treatments designed to rejuvenate the mind and body. Guests can enjoy a swim in the indoor pool, work out in the state-of-the-art fitness center, or simply unwind in the sauna.

For those interested in exploring Quebec City's rich history and culture, Château Frontenac's prime location in the heart of Old Quebec makes it an ideal base. The hotel is within walking distance of many of the city's most iconic landmarks, including the Plains of Abraham, the Citadelle, and the historic streets of Petit-Champlain. Guests can immerse themselves in the city's vibrant atmosphere, discovering its unique blend of French and Canadian influences.

Château Frontenac is also a hub of activity, hosting a variety of events and gatherings throughout the year. From elegant weddings and galas to business conferences and cultural festivals, the hotel's versatile event spaces accommodate a wide range of occasions. The Château's dedicated staff ensures that every event is executed with precision and style, creating unforgettable experiences for all who attend.

The hotel's commitment to preserving its heritage and embracing modernity is evident in its ongoing renovations and enhancements. Recent upgrades have blended contemporary design with historic elements, ensuring that Château Frontenac remains a premier destination for visitors seeking luxury and tradition.

Staying at Château Frontenac is more than just a hotel stay; it's an opportunity to become part of a legacy that has shaped the history of Quebec City. Guests are invited to step back in time and experience the grandeur and elegance that have defined the Château for over a century. Whether enjoying a sumptuous meal, exploring the city's historic sites, or simply relaxing in the comfort of their room, guests are enveloped in a world of sophistication and charm.

As night falls, the Château is illuminated, casting a warm glow over the city and river below. The sight of this majestic hotel, standing proudly against the night sky, is a reminder of its enduring place in the heart of Quebec City and the countless stories it holds within its walls. For those seeking a truly memorable experience, Château Frontenac offers a journey into the past, where history, luxury, and hospitality unite to create an unforgettable stay.

The Citadelle of Quebec: Fortifications and History

Dominating the landscape of Old Quebec, the Citadelle of Quebec stands as a formidable reminder of the city's strategic military significance. Nestled atop Cap Diamant, this star-shaped fortress offers a fascinating glimpse into the military history and architectural prowess that have defined Quebec City over centuries. As one of the largest British-built fortifications in North America, the Citadelle not only serves as an active military installation but also invites visitors to explore its storied past and impressive fortifications.

The Citadelle's history dates back to the early 19th century, a period marked by tension between British forces and American expansion. In response to the looming threat posed by the United States following the War of 1812, the British government initiated the construction of a defensive stronghold to protect the city of Quebec. The Citadelle was strategically positioned to control the St. Lawrence River, thereby safeguarding the vital waterway and the city itself. Its star-shaped design, inspired by the renowned French military engineer Sébastien Le Prestre de Vauban, provided enhanced defense capabilities against potential attacks.

A visit to the Citadelle begins with an ascent to its commanding location, where visitors are greeted by breathtaking views of the river and surrounding cityscape. The fortifications, constructed from local stone, exude an air of strength and permanence, their walls bearing witness to centuries of history. Guided tours are available, offering an in-depth look at the Citadelle's architecture, history, and ongoing role as a military base. Knowledgeable guides share insights into the fortress's design, its various defensive features, and the daily life of soldiers stationed there throughout history.

One of the most striking features of the Citadelle is the Governor General's residence, a stately building that serves as the official residence of the Governor General of Canada when in Quebec City. This residence, with its elegant architecture and beautifully landscaped gardens, reflects the Citadelle's dual role as both a military stronghold and a ceremonial site.

Visitors can explore the gardens and, on select occasions, tour the residence to gain a deeper understanding of its significance.

The Citadelle is also home to the Royal 22e Régiment, the only Francophone infantry regiment in the Canadian Armed Forces. This prestigious regiment, known as the "Van Doos," has a rich history of service and distinction. The regiment's museum, located within the Citadelle, showcases an extensive collection of artifacts, uniforms, and memorabilia that highlight its contributions to military history. The museum provides a comprehensive overview of the regiment's role in major conflicts, from World War I to peacekeeping missions around the globe.

Throughout the year, the Citadelle hosts a variety of events and ceremonies that celebrate its military heritage. The Changing of the Guard ceremony, a popular attraction during the summer months, offers a glimpse into military traditions as soldiers in full regalia perform their duties with precision and discipline. This daily ritual, accompanied by the stirring sounds of a military band, draws visitors from near and far, eager to witness the pageantry and history that the Citadelle embodies.

In addition to its historical and military significance, the Citadelle offers a unique perspective on the broader narrative of Quebec City. As a focal point of defense and governance, the fortress has played a pivotal role in shaping the city's identity and its relationship with the rest of Canada. The Citadelle's presence underscores Quebec City's strategic importance and its enduring legacy as a center of power and influence.

The Citadelle's importance extends beyond its walls, as it serves as a symbol of resilience and unity for the people of Quebec and Canada. Its enduring presence atop Cap Diamant speaks to the determination and ingenuity of those who built and defended it. As a living monument, the Citadelle continues to inspire pride and reflection, reminding visitors of the sacrifices and achievements that have defined the region's history.

For those interested in exploring the Citadelle's surroundings, the adjacent Plains of Abraham offer a serene and picturesque setting for walking, picnicking, or simply enjoying the natural beauty of the area. This historic battlefield, where the pivotal Battle of Quebec took place in 1759, has been transformed into a vast urban park that complements the Citadelle's historical significance.

The Citadelle of Quebec stands as a testament to the city's rich heritage and enduring spirit. Its fortifications, history, and ongoing role as a military base provide a fascinating glimpse into the past while offering a connection to the present. As visitors explore its storied walls and learn about the people and events that have shaped its history, they gain a deeper appreciation for the Citadelle's role in Quebec City's evolution. This iconic fortress not only tells the story of military strategy and defense but also embodies the resilience and pride of a city and its people.

The Plains of Abraham: Battlefields and Gardens

The Plains of Abraham, a vast expanse of rolling fields and manicured gardens, holds a place of profound historical significance in the heart of Quebec City. This iconic site, where the fate of New France was sealed in a decisive battle, is now a serene urban park that offers visitors a unique blend of history, beauty, and recreation. As you walk through these hallowed grounds, you are stepping into a landscape that has witnessed pivotal moments in the story of Canada.

In 1759, the Plains of Abraham became the stage for a battle that would alter the course of North American history. The Battle of Quebec, fought between the British forces led by General James Wolfe and the French troops commanded by General Louis-Joseph de Montcalm, was a short but fierce engagement. Lasting mere minutes, the battle culminated in a British victory, effectively ending French colonial rule in Canada and laying the groundwork for British dominance in the region.

The strategic significance of the Plains of Abraham lay in its geography. The open fields provided an ideal battleground for the British, who had made a daring ascent up the cliffs from the St. Lawrence River to surprise the French. The ensuing conflict, though brief, was brutal, resulting in the deaths of both Wolfe and Montcalm. This encounter marked a turning point in the Seven Years' War, with far-reaching implications for the future of Quebec and the entire continent.

Today, the Plains of Abraham bear little resemblance to the battlefield of the past. Instead, they have been transformed into one of North America's most beautiful urban parks, offering a peaceful retreat for residents and visitors alike. The park's expansive lawns and gardens create a tranquil oasis in the midst of the bustling city, providing a space for leisure, reflection, and cultural activities.

The park's transformation into a public space began in the early 20th century, when the city of Quebec recognized the need to preserve its historical legacy while providing a recreational area for its citizens. The development of the park was guided by a vision of blending history with nature, creating a landscape that honors the past while embracing the present.

Visitors to the Plains of Abraham can explore a wide array of attractions and activities. The park's walking trails offer a leisurely way to take in the natural beauty, with paths winding through gardens, wooded areas, and open fields. As you stroll along these trails, you may come across interpretive panels that provide insight into the historical events that unfolded here, offering a deeper understanding of the site's significance.

For those interested in delving deeper into the history of the Plains of Abraham, the Battlefields Park Museum offers a wealth of information and exhibits. Located within the park, the museum houses artifacts, maps, and displays that bring the story of the battle to life. Interactive exhibits allow visitors to experience the challenges faced by both the British and French forces, providing a vivid portrayal of the tactics and strategies employed during the conflict.

The park's gardens are a highlight for many visitors, showcasing a stunning array of flora that changes with the seasons. In spring, vibrant tulips and daffodils burst into bloom, creating a colorful spectacle that draws admirers from near and far. Summer brings lush greenery and fragrant roses, while autumn transforms the landscape into a tapestry of reds, oranges, and yellows. The gardens are meticulously maintained, providing a picturesque setting for picnics, photography, or simply enjoying the beauty of nature.

Throughout the year, the Plains of Abraham host a variety of events and activities that celebrate the cultural heritage of Quebec. From outdoor concerts and festivals to historical reenactments and guided tours, the park is a hub of activity that offers something for everyone. Winter brings its own charm, with the park's fields and trails transforming into a playground for cross-country skiing, snowshoeing, and sledding.

The Plains of Abraham also hold a special place in the hearts of Quebec City residents, serving as a gathering place for communal celebrations and commemorations. The park's open spaces provide the perfect backdrop for public events, from Canada Day festivities to cultural showcases that highlight the diverse traditions of the city.

For those seeking a moment of quiet reflection, the park offers numerous benches and secluded spots where you can sit and take in the views. Whether gazing at the majestic St. Lawrence River or contemplating the historic significance of the land beneath your feet, the Plains of Abraham invite you to connect with the past and present in a meaningful way.

As you explore the Plains of Abraham, you are walking in the footsteps of history, experiencing a place where the past continues to resonate. The park's beauty and tranquility belie the tumultuous events that once unfolded here, offering a powerful reminder of the resilience and strength of the people who have shaped its story. Through its landscapes and stories, the Plains of Abraham stand as a testament to the enduring legacy of Quebec City and its pivotal role in the history of Canada.

The Montmorency Falls: A Natural Wonder

Cascading majestically from a height of 83 meters, the Montmorency Falls present a breathtaking spectacle that captivates all who visit. Located just a short drive from Quebec City, this natural wonder surpasses even the famed Niagara Falls in height, offering an awe-inspiring display of nature's power and beauty. The falls are nestled within the Montmorency Falls Park, a picturesque area that invites exploration and adventure, making it a must-see destination for nature enthusiasts and thrill-seekers alike.

The Montmorency River, having carved its way through the rugged landscape, plunges dramatically over the cliff's edge to join the St. Lawrence River below. This powerful descent creates a misty spray and a thunderous roar that can be both seen and heard from afar. The falls are particularly striking during the spring thaw, when melting snow and ice swell the river, increasing the volume and intensity of the cascade.

A visit to Montmorency Falls offers a variety of ways to experience its grandeur. For those seeking an elevated perspective, a suspension bridge spans the top of the falls, providing stunning views of the torrent below and the surrounding landscape. The bridge offers a unique vantage point, allowing visitors to appreciate the sheer scale and power of the falls from above. As you stand on the bridge, the sensation of the rushing water beneath your feet is both exhilarating and humbling.

For a closer encounter, a staircase with over 480 steps descends along the cliff face, offering an up-close view of the falls as you make your way to the base. The descent is a journey in itself, with several lookout points along the way that provide opportunities to pause and take in the scenery. The fresh mist and the cool breeze from the falls add to the refreshing experience, making the climb back up a rewarding challenge for the adventurous.

The cable car ride is another popular way to explore the area, offering a leisurely ascent and descent with panoramic views of the falls, the park, and the Isle of Orleans in the distance. This aerial perspective highlights the natural beauty and diverse terrain of the region, with lush forests, rocky cliffs, and the ever-present roar of the falls creating a symphony of sights and sounds.

In winter, the Montmorency Falls undergo a magical transformation as the temperatures drop and the landscape becomes blanketed in snow and ice. The spray from the falls freezes upon contact, creating an impressive ice cone at the base, sometimes reaching up to 30 meters in height. This natural ice formation attracts ice climbers from around the world, eager to test their skills on the challenging frozen surface. The park is equally enchanting for those who prefer less extreme activities, offering trails for snowshoeing and winter walks that reveal the serene beauty of the frosted landscape.

Beyond their natural allure, the Montmorency Falls hold historical significance, having played a role in the military conflicts between the British and French during the 18th century. The falls were the site of the Battle of Montmorency in 1759, part of the larger campaign that culminated in the Battle of the Plains of Abraham. Historical markers and interpretive panels throughout the park provide context and insights into these events, enriching the visitor experience with stories from the past.

The surrounding parkland offers a wealth of recreational opportunities, making it an ideal destination for families and outdoor enthusiasts. Picnic areas provide the perfect setting for a leisurely meal amidst nature, while the park's trails beckon hikers and bikers to explore its diverse ecosystems. Whether you choose to embark on a guided tour or wander at your leisure, the park offers a chance to reconnect with nature and escape the bustle of urban life.

For those interested in capturing the perfect photograph, the Montmorency Falls provide endless opportunities to play with light, shadow, and motion. The falls' dynamic nature and ever-changing appearance, from the vibrant hues of autumn to the icy blues of winter, offer a rich canvas for photographers of all skill levels. Early morning and late afternoon light cast a warm glow on the landscape, while the falls' mist creates stunning rainbows that add an element of magic to any shot.

A visit to Montmorency Falls wouldn't be complete without indulging in the local culinary delights. The park's restaurant, strategically located with views of the falls, serves a menu of Quebecois specialties that highlight the region's rich culinary heritage. Savor dishes made with fresh local ingredients, from hearty poutine to delicate maple-infused desserts, as you relax and soak in the beauty of your surroundings.

Whether you're seeking adventure, relaxation, or a deeper connection with history and nature, Montmorency Falls offers an unforgettable experience. Its majestic presence and the surrounding parklands provide an inspiring backdrop for exploration and discovery, inviting visitors to immerse themselves in the wonders of the natural world. As you stand before the falls, you'll find yourself captivated by their power and beauty, a testament to the timeless allure of nature's creations.

Quartier Petit Champlain: Cobblestone Streets and Boutiques

Nestled at the foot of Cap Diamant, Quartier Petit Champlain beckons with its cobblestone streets, charming boutiques, and vibrant atmosphere. This enchanting neighborhood, part of Old Quebec, is one of North America's oldest commercial districts. Steeped in history and brimming with character, Petit Champlain is a delightful blend of the past and present, where visitors can lose themselves in a maze of narrow lanes lined with quaint shops, cafes, and galleries.

Walking through Petit Champlain is akin to stepping into a European village, with its historical architecture and intimate streetscapes creating an ambiance that is both romantic and inviting. The district's origins date back to the early days of

New France, when it served as a bustling center of trade and commerce. Today, it retains much of its old-world charm, drawing visitors from around the world eager to experience its unique allure.

The heart of Petit Champlain is Rue du Petit-Champlain, a pedestrian street that meanders through the neighborhood, offering a feast for the senses. As you stroll along this picturesque thoroughfare, you are greeted by the aroma of freshly baked pastries wafting from cozy bakeries, the sound of street musicians filling the air with melody, and the sight of colorful storefronts adorned with flowers and seasonal decorations. The street is a living tapestry of sights and sounds, inviting exploration and discovery at every turn.

Boutiques in Petit Champlain are a testament to the area's artistic flair and creativity. From handmade crafts and artisanal goods to designer clothing and unique souvenirs, the shops offer a diverse array of treasures waiting to be uncovered. Each boutique has its own story and character, reflecting the passion and craftsmanship of local artisans and entrepreneurs. Whether you're searching for a one-of-a-kind piece of jewelry, a lovingly crafted piece of pottery, or a stylish accessory, Petit Champlain's boutiques promise a shopping experience like no other.

Art galleries in the neighborhood showcase the talent and vision of both established and emerging artists. Visitors can explore a variety of styles and mediums, from contemporary paintings and sculptures to traditional Quebecois art. These galleries not only provide a platform for artists to share their work but also offer a glimpse into the cultural heartbeat of the region. Art lovers will find themselves captivated by the diverse range of creativity on display, with each gallery offering a unique perspective on the artistic landscape.

For those seeking a taste of Quebec's culinary delights, Petit Champlain's cafes and restaurants provide an array of tempting options. Whether you're in the mood for a leisurely brunch, a hearty lunch, or a romantic dinner, the district's dining establishments cater to every palate. Cozy bistros serve up classic Quebecois dishes, from tourtière to poutine, while elegant restaurants offer gourmet cuisine that celebrates the region's rich culinary heritage. As you savor each bite, you'll find yourself immersed in the flavors and traditions that define Quebec's gastronomy.

Petit Champlain's theaters and performance venues add to the district's vibrant cultural scene. Whether you're attending a live music performance, a theatrical production, or a local festival, the neighborhood offers a wealth of entertainment options that enrich the visitor experience. The area's commitment to the arts is evident in the diverse range of events and performances that take place throughout the year, providing a dynamic backdrop to the district's historical charm.

Seasonal festivals and celebrations bring an added layer of magic to Petit Champlain, transforming the neighborhood into a festive wonderland. During the winter months, the district is adorned with twinkling lights and holiday decorations, creating a scene straight out of a fairy tale. The annual Carnaval de Québec, one of the world's largest winter festivals, sees the streets come alive with parades, ice sculptures, and joyous revelry. In the summer, outdoor concerts and street performances fill the air with music and laughter, inviting visitors to join in the festivities.

Petit Champlain's historical significance is also celebrated through its architecture, with many buildings dating back to the 17th and 18th centuries. These well-preserved structures offer a window into the past, telling the story of the district's evolution from a bustling port to a thriving cultural hub. The Maison Chevalier, a historic house museum, provides an opportunity to delve deeper into the area's heritage, offering exhibits and guided tours that explore the lives of the people who once called Petit Champlain home.

A visit to Petit Champlain is incomplete without a ride on the Old Quebec Funicular, which connects the neighborhood to the Upper Town. This unique mode of transportation not only offers a convenient way to traverse the steep incline but also provides stunning views of the St. Lawrence River and the surrounding cityscape. As you ascend or descend, you'll gain a new perspective on the beauty and charm of Quebec City, with Petit Champlain nestled comfortably at its heart.

The district's intimate size and pedestrian-friendly layout make it easy to explore at your own pace, allowing you to fully immerse yourself in its charm and character. Whether you're wandering the cobblestone streets, browsing the eclectic boutiques, or savoring a delicious meal, Petit Champlain offers an experience that is both enchanting and unforgettable. It is a place where history and modernity coexist in harmony, creating a vibrant tapestry of culture and tradition that leaves a lasting impression.

Quartier Petit Champlain stands as a testament to the enduring spirit and creativity of Quebec City. Its cobblestone streets and boutique-lined avenues invite visitors to step back in time while celebrating the present, offering a unique glimpse into the soul of the city. As you explore this magical neighborhood, you'll find yourself enchanted by its beauty, inspired by its creativity, and connected to its rich history, all of which come together to create an extraordinary journey through one of Quebec's most beloved districts.

Dufferin Terrace: Panoramic Views of the St. Lawrence River

Stretching gracefully along the edge of Old Quebec, Dufferin Terrace offers visitors an unparalleled panorama of the St. Lawrence River, creating a scenic promenade imbued with history and charm. This iconic boardwalk, nestled between the historic Château Frontenac and the cascading cliffs of Cap Diamant, serves as a gathering place where the city's past and present merge against a backdrop of stunning natural beauty.

Dufferin Terrace owes its name to Lord Dufferin, a former Governor General of Canada, whose vision helped preserve Quebec City's fortifications and enhance its cultural heritage. His influence is evident in the terrace's elegant design and its role as a beloved public space. Originally constructed in the late 19th century, the boardwalk has since become a focal point of the city's social and cultural life, drawing visitors and locals alike to its wide expanse for leisurely strolls, breathtaking views, and vibrant events.

As you set foot on Dufferin Terrace, the sweeping vistas of the St. Lawrence River immediately capture your attention. The river, a vital artery in Canada's history, flows majestically below, its waters reflecting the changing hues of the sky. On clear days, the vista extends across to the distant Isle of Orleans and beyond, offering a captivating view that shifts with the seasons. In spring and summer, the riverbank bursts into verdant life, while autumn paints the landscape in warm tones of red and gold. Even winter has its charm, with the river's icy expanse shimmering under a blanket of snow.

The terrace's wooden planks, polished smooth by countless footsteps, invite exploration. The gentle curve of the boardwalk leads visitors past ornate gazebos and lampposts, evoking a sense of timeless elegance. Benches line the promenade, offering spots to pause and drink in the scenery or simply enjoy the lively atmosphere. Street performers often grace the terrace with music and entertainment, adding a lively rhythm to the gentle murmur of conversation and the distant call of river birds.

Dominating one end of Dufferin Terrace stands the Château Frontenac, an architectural masterpiece that has become synonymous with Quebec City itself. This grand hotel, with its towering turrets and copper roofs, lends an air of regal splendor to the boardwalk. As you stroll past its façade, you can almost hear echoes of the past—the distant clatter of horse-drawn carriages, the rustle of elegant gowns, and the laughter of guests who have graced its halls over the decades.

The terrace also serves as a gateway to the city's rich history. At its heart lies the archaeological site of Saint-Louis Forts and

Châteaux, where visitors can explore the remains of the original French fortifications that once stood here. Guided tours and interpretive panels offer insights into the strategic importance of this location, providing a glimpse into the lives of the early settlers who defended Quebec against foreign incursions. The site is a poignant reminder of the city's resilience and the enduring legacy of its founders.

Throughout the year, Dufferin Terrace plays host to a variety of events and celebrations that showcase the vibrant culture of Quebec City. In summer, the terrace comes alive with festivals and concerts, transforming the boardwalk into an open-air stage that pulses with energy and excitement. The annual Quebec Summer Festival, a highlight of the cultural calendar, brings renowned musicians and performers to the city, drawing large crowds to the terrace for unforgettable evenings of music and dance.

During the winter months, Dufferin Terrace takes on a magical quality as it becomes part of the Quebec Winter Carnival. The terrace is adorned with ice sculptures and festive decorations, creating a winter wonderland that delights visitors of all ages. The toboggan slide, a beloved tradition, offers an exhilarating descent down the terrace, with riders enjoying a thrilling ride against the backdrop of the snowy landscape. The carnival's lively atmosphere and joyful spirit infuse the terrace with warmth and camaraderie, even on the coldest days.

For those seeking a more contemplative experience, Dufferin Terrace offers numerous opportunities for reflection and relaxation. The gentle flow of the river, the soft rustle of leaves, and the distant hum of the city create a serene ambiance that invites introspection. As the sun sets and the sky transforms into a canvas of vibrant colors, the terrace becomes a place of quiet beauty, where one can lose track of time and simply be present in the moment.

Dufferin Terrace is also a starting point for exploring the surrounding historic district of Old Quebec. The nearby Funicular Railway provides a convenient link to Lower Town, offering a scenic ride between the two levels of the city. From here, visitors can wander the charming streets of Petit Champlain or explore the shops and cafes that line the narrow lanes of Old Quebec, each turn revealing new discoveries and delightful surprises.

As you bid farewell to Dufferin Terrace, you'll carry with you memories of its captivating views and vibrant atmosphere—a place where history and nature coexist in perfect harmony. The terrace stands as a testament to Quebec City's enduring spirit, a place where the stories of the past continue to weave into the fabric of the present. It's a space that invites you to pause, to savor each moment, and to celebrate the beauty of a city that has long been a beacon of culture and heritage.

CHAPTER 4: CULTURAL FESTIVALS AND EVENTS

Montreal Jazz Festival: A Celebration of Sound

Montreal Jazz Festival, an electrifying celebration of sound and rhythm, transforms the city into a vibrant musical haven each year. As one of the world's largest and most prestigious jazz festivals, it draws artists and audiences from across the globe, turning the heart of Montreal into a pulsating epicenter of music and culture. This iconic festival, which began in 1980, has grown exponentially, now featuring an impressive lineup of performances that span a multitude of genres and styles, all rooted in the rich tradition of jazz.

Wandering through the festival's sprawling outdoor venues, one is immediately enveloped by the pulsating energy that permeates every corner of the city. Stages are set up in various public spaces, from the sprawling Place des Festivals to intimate street corners, creating a dynamic tapestry of sound that echoes through the urban landscape. The festival's unique ability to blend world-class talent with local charm makes it a truly immersive experience, inviting attendees to embark on a journey of musical discovery.

The diversity of the festival's lineup is staggering, showcasing both legendary icons and emerging artists who push the boundaries of jazz and its related genres. From traditional jazz ensembles and big bands to contemporary fusion acts and avant-garde experimentalists, the festival offers a kaleidoscope of sounds that cater to every musical taste. It's not uncommon to find yourself grooving to a soulful saxophone solo one moment, only to be swept away by the intricate rhythms of a Latin jazz ensemble the next.

Beyond the music, the festival serves as a cultural melting pot, bringing together people from all walks of life to celebrate their shared love of jazz. The streets come alive with the vibrant colors of festival-goers, their laughter and chatter mingling with the melodies that fill the air. Food stalls and artisan vendors line the festival grounds, offering a taste of Montreal's diverse culinary scene and providing a feast for the senses that complements the auditory delights.

Interactive workshops and masterclasses add an educational dimension to the festival, offering budding musicians and enthusiasts the chance to learn from the masters. These sessions provide invaluable insights into the art of jazz, covering everything from improvisation techniques and instrumental proficiency to the history and evolution of the genre. Attendees have the opportunity to engage in lively discussions, share their own experiences, and gain a deeper appreciation for the intricacies of jazz music.

A highlight of the festival is its commitment to nurturing new talent, providing a platform for emerging artists to showcase their skills and gain exposure on an international stage. The festival's various competitions and showcases are fiercely contested, with participants vying for the chance to launch their careers and make their mark in the world of jazz. This nurturing of young talent ensures that the festival remains vibrant and relevant, constantly infusing new energy and ideas into its programming.

Evenings during the festival are magical, as the city is bathed in the warm glow of stage lights, casting a golden hue over the throngs of music lovers gathered to witness unforgettable performances. The atmosphere is electric, with an air of anticipation and excitement palpable in the crowd. As the sun sets and the music takes center stage, time seems to stand still, and the worries of the world fade away, replaced by the pure joy of musical expression.

The festival's influence extends beyond its annual celebration, leaving a lasting impact on the cultural landscape of Montreal. It has played a pivotal role in establishing the city as a global hub for jazz, attracting visitors year-round who seek to explore its rich musical heritage. Local musicians and venues thrive in its wake, inspired by the festival's success and eager to contribute to the city's vibrant jazz scene.

For those who have experienced the magic of the Montreal Jazz Festival, it becomes a cherished memory, a reminder of the transformative power of music to unite and uplift. It is a testament to the enduring legacy of jazz, a genre that has transcended boundaries and brought people together for generations. The festival is more than just a series of concerts; it is a celebration of creativity, diversity, and the shared human experience.

As the final notes of the festival fade into the night, the city of Montreal is left with a lingering sense of camaraderie and connection. The memories created during this time will resonate long after the stages are dismantled and the crowds disperse. The Montreal Jazz Festival stands as a beacon of artistic innovation and cultural collaboration, a testament to the universal language of music and its power to transcend differences and bring people together in harmony.

Quebec Winter Carnival: Snow, Ice, and Laughter

Every year, as the crisp winter air settles over Quebec City, the streets come alive with the sounds of laughter and celebration, heralding the arrival of the Quebec Winter Carnival. This iconic festival, known as the largest winter carnival in the world, transforms the city into a vibrant playground of snow and ice, attracting visitors from near and far to partake in its joyous festivities. With its rich history and diverse array of activities, the carnival is a testament to the enduring spirit of the Quebecois, who embrace the cold with warmth and enthusiasm.

The roots of the Quebec Winter Carnival stretch back to the late 19th century, when the city first hosted a winter festival to combat the doldrums of the long, harsh season. Over the years, the carnival has evolved into a grand celebration of winter's beauty and challenges, inviting people of all ages to revel in the magic of the season. The carnival's mascot, Bonhomme, a jolly snowman with a red cap and sash, embodies the spirit of the event, welcoming everyone with open arms and a contagious smile.

One of the carnival's most beloved traditions is the construction of the Ice Palace, a stunning architectural marvel made entirely of ice. Set against the backdrop of the city, this shimmering structure serves as the focal point of the festivities, hosting concerts, performances, and events throughout the carnival's duration. At night, the palace is illuminated with colorful lights, casting a magical glow that enchants all who behold it.

Visitors to the carnival can enjoy a wide range of activities that celebrate the unique joys of winter. The snow-covered Plains of Abraham become a hub of excitement, offering opportunities for snowshoeing, cross-country skiing, and sledding. Families can delight in the thrill of the toboggan run, racing down the hill with the wind in their hair and laughter ringing in their ears. For those seeking a more leisurely experience, horse-drawn sleigh rides provide a charming way to explore the wintry landscape, with the gentle jingle of sleigh bells adding to the festive atmosphere.

The International Snow Sculpture Competition is a highlight of the carnival, showcasing the incredible talent and creativity of artists from around the world. These sculptors transform blocks of snow into breathtaking works of art, each piece telling a unique story through intricate details and imaginative designs. As visitors wander through this open-air gallery, they are transported to a world of wonder and whimsy, where snow and ice become the medium for artistic expression.

No winter carnival would be complete without a parade, and Quebec's is a spectacle like no other. The Night Parades light up the streets with colorful floats, marching bands, and performers, creating a lively atmosphere that captivates audiences of all ages. The processions wind their way through the city, spreading cheer and delight as they go, with Bonhomme himself often leading the way, waving to the crowds and spreading his infectious joy.

The carnival's culinary offerings are a feast for the senses, with vendors serving up a delectable array of traditional Quebecois dishes and seasonal treats. From hearty poutine and tourtière to sweet maple taffy and hot chocolate, there is something to satisfy every craving. The warmth of these comforting foods provides a welcome respite from the cold, inviting visitors to indulge in the region's rich gastronomic heritage.

For those with a competitive spirit, the carnival offers a variety of games and challenges that test both skill and endurance. The Canoe Race on the icy waters of the St. Lawrence River is a thrilling event that pits teams against the elements, requiring strength, teamwork, and determination to reach the finish line. The Ice Canoe Race is another exhilarating competition, where participants navigate a course of ice floes and open water, showcasing their prowess and resilience.

The carnival also places a strong emphasis on family-friendly activities, ensuring that even the youngest visitors can join in the fun. From face painting and storytelling to puppet shows and interactive workshops, there are plenty of options to keep children entertained and engaged. The carnival's inclusive atmosphere encourages families to create lasting memories together, fostering a sense of community and connection that is at the heart of the event.

As the carnival draws to a close, the city bids farewell to another year of winter wonder with a grand fireworks display that lights up the night sky. This dazzling show of color and light is a fitting finale to the festivities, leaving spectators in awe and anticipation for the next edition of the carnival.

The Quebec Winter Carnival is more than just a celebration of snow and ice; it is a testament to the indomitable spirit of the people who call this place home. It is a reminder that even in the coldest months, warmth and laughter can bring people together, creating a sense of joy and camaraderie that transcends the chill. For those who experience its magic, the carnival leaves an indelible mark, a cherished memory of a time when winter's embrace was met with open arms and hearts filled with laughter.

Montreal's Just for Laughs Festival: Comedy's Biggest Stage

In the heart of summer, Montreal transforms into the world capital of comedy as it hosts the renowned Just for Laughs Festival. This iconic event, the largest international comedy festival, unfolds across the city's vibrant streets and venues, drawing comedians and audiences from around the globe. With its roots dating back to 1983, the festival has become a cornerstone of Montreal's cultural identity, offering a stage where laughter reigns supreme and humor knows no bounds.

The festival's allure lies in its eclectic lineup, featuring a dazzling array of comedic talent that spans genres and styles. From stand-up and sketch comedy to improv and theatrical performances, the festival showcases both established icons and emerging stars, each bringing their unique brand of humor to the stage. As you navigate the bustling festival grounds, the infectious energy of performers and spectators alike creates an atmosphere that is both electric and welcoming.

The streets of Montreal come alive with laughter as the city becomes a playground for comedic expression. Outdoor stages and pop-up performances invite passersby to pause and enjoy impromptu shows, transforming everyday spaces into sites of hilarity and surprise. Street performers, clad in colorful costumes, engage audiences with their antics, blurring the line between performer and spectator in a delightful dance of spontaneous comedy.

At the heart of the festival are its gala shows, grand spectacles that feature a roster of top-tier comedians from around the world. These star-studded events, often hosted by celebrated figures in the comedy scene, offer audiences a chance to witness the best in the business deliver side-splitting performances that leave no topic untouched. The gala shows are a highlight of the festival, combining theatrical flair with comedic brilliance to create unforgettable evenings of entertainment.

Beyond the glitz and glamour of the gala shows, the festival also serves as an incubator for new talent, providing a platform for up-and-coming comedians to hone their craft and gain exposure. The festival's New Faces showcase is a highly anticipated event, where emerging comedians take the stage before industry professionals and enthusiastic crowds, hoping to make their mark in the world of comedy. This commitment to nurturing fresh talent ensures the festival remains dynamic and forward-thinking, continually evolving with the ever-changing landscape of comedy.

Workshops and panel discussions add an educational dimension to the festival, offering aspiring comedians and comedy enthusiasts insights into the intricacies of the craft. These sessions delve into topics such as writing techniques, comedic timing, and the business of comedy, providing valuable knowledge and fostering a deeper appreciation for the art form. Attendees have the opportunity to engage with seasoned professionals, ask questions, and learn from their experiences, making these events an integral part of the festival experience.

The festival's influence extends beyond the stage, permeating the city's cultural fabric and leaving a lasting impact on Montreal's vibrant arts scene. Local comedy clubs and venues thrive in its wake, inspired by the festival's success and eager to contribute to the city's reputation as a comedic hub. The festival's legacy is evident in the thriving community of comedians and performers who call Montreal home, each adding their voice to the city's rich tapestry of humor.

For those fortunate enough to experience the Just for Laughs Festival, it becomes a cherished memory, a testament to the transformative power of laughter to unite and uplift. It is a celebration of comedy in all its forms, a reminder that humor transcends language and culture, bringing people together in moments of shared joy and connection. The festival is more than just a series of performances; it is a testament to the enduring appeal of comedy and its ability to reflect the human experience with wit and wisdom.

As the festival draws to a close, the echoes of laughter linger in the air, a reminder of the joy and camaraderie that define this extraordinary event. The Just for Laughs Festival stands as a beacon of creativity and innovation, a testament to the universal language of comedy and its power to transcend differences and bring people together in harmony. For Montreal, it is a celebration of the city's vibrant spirit and a testament to its enduring status as a global capital of humor.

Fête de la Nouvelle-France: Quebec City's Historical Celebration

Quebec City, with its cobblestone streets and historic architecture, offers a perfect backdrop for the Fête de la Nouvelle-France, a captivating festival that brings the past to life with vivid color and vibrant energy. This annual celebration, steeped in history, invites locals and visitors to step back in time and experience the rich heritage of New France, the early French settlements in North America. The festival transforms the city into a living museum, where history is not just remembered but actively celebrated.

The Fête de la Nouvelle-France originated in 1997, conceived to commemorate and honor the founding of Quebec City and the broader historical period of New France, which spanned from the early 16th century to the mid-18th century. Each August, the city is filled with the sights and sounds of the past as participants don period costumes, and the air echoes with the melodies of traditional music. The festival is a joyous reminder of the cultural roots that have shaped Quebec's unique identity.

Visitors to the Fête de la Nouvelle-France are immediately immersed in a world where history and imagination converge. The streets of Old Quebec become a stage for a grand pageantry of historical reenactments, parades, and performances. Actors portraying historical figures and everyday citizens of New France roam the city, bringing to life the stories of explorers, merchants, and indigenous peoples who played pivotal roles in the region's history. Through these encounters, festival-goers gain a deeper understanding of the challenges and triumphs faced by the early settlers.

Traditional music and dance are at the heart of the festival, offering a lively soundtrack to the historical festivities. From lively folk tunes played on fiddles and accordions to elegant courtly dances, the music reflects the diverse cultural influences that have shaped Quebec over the centuries. Dance performances often invite audience participation, encouraging visitors to join in the revelry and experience the joy of communal celebration. The rhythms of the past resonate with a contemporary audience, bridging the gap between history and modernity.

The festival's culinary offerings provide another avenue for exploring the flavors and traditions of New France. Local chefs and vendors serve up an array of historical dishes, from tourtière and pea soup to maple treats and freshly baked bread. These culinary delights offer a taste of the past, allowing festival-goers to savor the same flavors that would have graced the tables of early settlers. The emphasis on locally sourced ingredients and traditional preparation methods highlights the enduring connection between Quebec's culinary heritage and its agricultural roots.

Craft and trade demonstrations are a staple of the festival, showcasing the skills and craftsmanship that were vital to life in New France. Artisans demonstrate techniques such as blacksmithing, weaving, and woodworking, offering a glimpse into the daily lives of the settlers. These hands-on activities provide an engaging way for visitors to learn about the ingenuity and resourcefulness that defined the era. The demonstrations serve as a reminder of the importance of preserving traditional crafts and skills for future generations.

The Fête de la Nouvelle-France also places a strong emphasis on the role of indigenous cultures in the history of Quebec. The festival celebrates the contributions and traditions of the indigenous peoples who inhabited the land long before the arrival of European settlers. Through storytelling, music, and art, indigenous performers and artists share their rich cultural heritage, fostering a spirit of respect and understanding among festival participants. This inclusive approach highlights the interconnectedness of the diverse cultures that have shaped the region's history.

Throughout the festival, educational exhibits and workshops provide opportunities for deeper exploration of the historical period. Scholars and historians offer lectures and guided tours, shedding light on the social, economic, and political dynamics of New France. These educational components enrich the festival experience, offering insights into the complex tapestry of history that has shaped Quebec's cultural landscape. Participants leave with a greater appreciation for the struggles and achievements of those who laid the foundations of modern-day Quebec.

The festival's grand parade is a highlight of the event, drawing large crowds to witness a spectacular procession of floats, musicians, and costumed participants. Each float represents a different aspect of life in New France, from exploration and trade to agriculture and religion. The parade is a visual feast, capturing the imagination with its vivid colors and intricate detail. As it winds through the streets of Old Quebec, the parade embodies the spirit of celebration and unity that defines the Fête de la Nouvelle-France.

For both residents and visitors, the festival is an opportunity to connect with Quebec's rich historical heritage in a tangible and meaningful way. It serves as a reminder of the enduring influence of New France on the cultural identity of the region, celebrating the legacy of those who came before. The festival fosters a sense of pride and belonging, inviting participants to reflect on the past while looking toward the future.

As the Fête de la Nouvelle-France comes to a close, the echoes of music and laughter linger in the air, leaving behind a sense of connection and continuity with the past. The festival is more than just a historical reenactment; it is a celebration of the spirit and resilience of the people who have shaped Quebec's unique heritage. Through the lens of history, the festival invites us to appreciate the richness of our shared cultural journey and to cherish the stories that continue to define us.

Montreal Pride: A Vibrant and Colorful Event

Montreal Pride, known locally as Fierté Montréal, stands as a beacon of inclusivity and celebration, embracing the diversity that defines the city's LGBTQ+ community. Every summer, the streets of Montreal burst into a riot of color and sound, drawing visitors from all walks of life to join in the festivities. With its roots in the struggle for equality and acceptance, Montreal Pride has evolved into one of the largest and most vibrant pride festivals in North America, offering a platform for expression, advocacy, and unity.

The origins of Montreal Pride can be traced back to the late 1970s, a time when the LGBTQ+ community was beginning to find its voice in the face of discrimination and prejudice. Over the years, the festival has grown exponentially, reflecting the increasing visibility and acceptance of LGBTQ+ individuals in society. Today, Montreal Pride is a ten-day extravaganza, featuring a diverse array of events that celebrate the unique contributions of the LGBTQ+ community to the cultural fabric of the city.

As the festival kicks off, the city is transformed into a vibrant tapestry of rainbow flags, banners, and decorations. The air is filled with excitement and anticipation as people gather to celebrate love, diversity, and equality. The festival's programming is as diverse as its participants, offering something for everyone, from lively parades and concerts to thoughtful panel discussions and workshops.

The Pride Parade is the centerpiece of the festival, a joyous procession that winds its way through the heart of the city. Participants, adorned in colorful costumes and carrying banners emblazoned with messages of love and acceptance, march proudly down the streets, cheered on by enthusiastic crowds. The parade is a celebration of identity and unity, a powerful reminder of the progress that has been made in the fight for LGBTQ+ rights and the work that still lies ahead.

Music plays a central role in the festival, with stages set up across the city hosting an eclectic lineup of performances. From pop and rock to electronic and hip-hop, the festival's musical offerings cater to a wide range of tastes, ensuring that there is something for everyone to enjoy. Local and international artists alike take to the stage, their performances infusing the city with an infectious energy that resonates with audiences long after the last note has been played.

In addition to music, the festival features a variety of cultural events that highlight the artistic talents of the LGBTQ+ community. Art exhibitions, film screenings, and theater performances provide a platform for queer artists to share their work and tell their stories. These events offer a space for reflection and dialogue, encouraging audiences to engage with the themes of identity, resilience, and empowerment that are central to the LGBTQ+ experience.

Workshops and panel discussions add an educational dimension to the festival, offering participants the opportunity to learn about the challenges facing the LGBTQ+ community and the ways in which they can contribute to positive change. Topics range from health and wellness to advocacy and activism, providing valuable insights and fostering a sense of solidarity among attendees. These sessions serve as a reminder that pride is not just about celebration, but also about education and empowerment.

One of the festival's standout features is its commitment to inclusivity and accessibility. Efforts are made to ensure that all events are welcoming and accessible to people of all abilities and backgrounds, creating a space where everyone can feel safe and supported. This commitment is reflected in the diverse range of events on offer, which cater to different interests, identities, and experiences within the LGBTQ+ spectrum.

Family-friendly activities are also an integral part of the festival, inviting people of all ages to join in the celebrations. From storytelling sessions and craft workshops to family picnics and play areas, the festival offers a wealth of options for families to enjoy together. These activities emphasize the importance of creating a supportive and inclusive environment for LGBTQ+ families and allies, fostering a sense of community and connection across generations.

As the sun sets on the festival, the city becomes a playground for nightlife enthusiasts, with parties and events taking place in venues across Montreal. Clubs and bars open their doors to revelers, offering a variety of themed nights and special performances that keep the celebrations going into the early hours. The nightlife scene is a testament to Montreal's reputation as a city that knows how to celebrate, offering a space for people to let loose and embrace their authentic selves.

Montreal Pride is more than just a festival; it is a celebration of love, diversity, and resilience. It is a testament to the strength and solidarity of the LGBTQ+ community and its allies, a reminder of the power of unity and the importance of standing together in the face of adversity. For those who attend, the festival is an opportunity to connect with others, to celebrate who they are, and to be part of a movement that continues to champion equality and acceptance for all.

As the festival draws to a close, the echoes of laughter and music linger in the air, leaving behind a sense of hope and inspiration. Montreal Pride stands as a beacon of progress and possibility, a celebration of the journey that has been traveled and the path that lies ahead. Through the lens of pride, the festival invites us to embrace our differences, to celebrate our shared humanity, and to continue working towards a world where everyone is free to live and love without fear or prejudice.

The Festival d'été de Québec: Quebec City's Summer Music Extravaganza

Each year, as the warmth of summer envelops Quebec City, the Festival d'été de Québec emerges as a beacon of musical celebration, drawing enthusiasts from all corners of the globe. This ten-day extravaganza, one of the largest music festivals in Canada, transforms the city's historic heart into a vibrant soundscape, where genres collide and musical magic unfolds. From rock and pop to jazz and classical, the festival's diverse lineup ensures that there is something for every musical palate, offering an immersive experience that transcends borders and unites audiences through the universal language of music.

The festival's origins date back to 1968, when a group of young visionaries sought to create a cultural event that would breathe new life into the city during the summer months. Over the years, the Festival d'été de Québec has grown exponentially, becoming a cornerstone of the city's cultural identity and a must-attend event on the international music calendar. Its success lies in its ability to adapt and innovate, continually curating a lineup that balances international superstars with emerging talent, ensuring that each edition of the festival is both fresh and familiar.

As the festival kicks off, Quebec City's streets and parks come alive with the sounds of music and laughter. The iconic Plains of Abraham serves as the festival's main stage, a sprawling outdoor venue that offers breathtaking views of the city and its surroundings. It is here that some of the world's biggest musical acts deliver electrifying performances, their sounds echoing across the plains and drawing enthusiastic crowds who gather to witness musical history in the making.

Beyond the main stage, the festival extends to various venues throughout the city, each offering its own unique atmosphere and lineup. Intimate clubs, historic theaters, and bustling street corners become stages for artists of all genres, creating a dynamic tapestry of sound that permeates the city. This decentralized approach allows festival-goers to explore Quebec City's rich cultural landscape while discovering new music along the way.

One of the festival's defining features is its commitment to showcasing a diverse array of musical genres. While the main stage may host chart-topping pop and rock acts, other venues offer a smorgasbord of musical styles, from jazz and blues to world music and electronic. This eclectic mix ensures that there is always something new and exciting to discover, inviting audiences to step outside their musical comfort zones and embrace the unexpected.

The festival also places a strong emphasis on promoting local talent, providing a platform for Quebec's burgeoning music scene to shine on a global stage. Local artists and bands are featured prominently throughout the festival, offering audiences a chance to experience the vibrant creativity and innovation that defines Quebec's musical landscape. This celebration of homegrown talent not only supports the local music industry but also showcases the province's rich cultural heritage to a wider audience.

For those seeking a break from the music, the festival offers a variety of cultural activities and attractions that highlight Quebec City's unique charm. Art installations, street performances, and culinary events provide a feast for the senses, inviting festival-goers to immerse themselves in the city's vibrant atmosphere. The festival's family-friendly programming ensures that there is something for attendees of all ages to enjoy, fostering a sense of community and connection that is at the heart of the event.

Workshops and masterclasses add an educational dimension to the festival, offering aspiring musicians and enthusiasts the opportunity to learn from industry professionals. These sessions cover a broad range of topics, from songwriting and production techniques to the business of music, providing valuable insights and inspiration for those looking to pursue a career in the industry. The festival's commitment to education and mentorship underscores its role as a catalyst for artistic growth and development.

As night falls, the festival's energy reaches a crescendo, with the city's venues and streets pulsating with music and excitement. The vibrant nightlife scene offers a variety of options for those looking to continue the celebrations, from late-night concerts and DJ sets to impromptu jam sessions and open mic nights. This nocturnal energy is a testament to Quebec City's reputation as a city that knows how to celebrate, offering a space for people to come together and revel in the joy of music.

The Festival d'été de Québec is more than just a series of concerts; it is a celebration of the transformative power of music to unite and inspire. It is a testament to the enduring appeal of live performance and the unique connection that is forged between artists and audiences. For those who attend, the festival is an opportunity to experience the magic of music in a setting that is both historic and contemporary, offering a glimpse into the rich cultural tapestry that defines Quebec City.

As the festival draws to a close, the echoes of music linger in the air, leaving behind a sense of joy and fulfillment. The Festival d'été de Québec stands as a beacon of creativity and innovation, a celebration of the shared human experience that music so beautifully encapsulates. Through the lens of the festival, we are reminded of the power of music to transcend barriers, to connect us to one another, and to inspire us to dream big and embrace the possibilities that lie ahead.

Navigating the Festival Calendar: How to Plan Your Visit

Planning a visit to Quebec's vibrant festival scene is an exciting endeavor, offering a chance to immerse oneself in a rich tapestry of cultural events and experiences. With a diverse array of festivals occurring throughout the year, each showcasing a unique facet of Quebec's cultural identity, the challenge lies in navigating the festival calendar to maximize your experience. Whether you're drawn to the dazzling lights of the Winter Carnival or the pulsating rhythms of the Summer Music Extravaganza, careful planning can enhance your visit and ensure you make the most of your time in this enchanting province.

Begin by familiarizing yourself with the festival calendar, which spans the entire year and encompasses a wide range of events. Quebec's festivals are as diverse as they are numerous, celebrating everything from music and art to history and gastronomy. To make informed decisions, research the festivals that align with your interests and preferences. Consider what you hope to experience, whether it's the thrill of live performances, the joy of culinary exploration, or the allure of historical reenactments. With this information in hand, you can begin to prioritize the festivals that resonate most with you.

Once you've identified the festivals you'd like to attend, it's important to consider the timing of your visit. Quebec's climate varies significantly throughout the year, with each season offering its own distinct charm. Winter festivals, such as the Quebec Winter Carnival, embrace the cold with snow-covered landscapes and ice sculptures, while summer events, like the Festival d'été de Québec, celebrate the warmth with outdoor concerts and street performances. Understanding the seasonal context of each festival will help you pack appropriately and make the most of your experience.

As you plan your visit, keep in mind the logistics of traveling to and within Quebec. The province's major cities, including Montreal and Quebec City, are well-connected by air, rail, and road, making it relatively easy to reach your desired destinations. Once you've arrived, consider the most convenient mode of transportation for navigating the city and accessing festival venues. Public transit is a popular choice, offering an affordable and efficient way to explore urban areas. Alternatively, renting a bicycle or using ride-sharing services can provide flexibility and convenience, particularly if you're attending events spread across different locations.

Accommodation is another key consideration when planning your festival visit. Quebec's cities offer a wide range of lodging options, from luxury hotels to budget-friendly hostels and charming bed-and-breakfasts. When selecting accommodations, consider their proximity to festival venues and public transportation, as well as any special amenities or services that may enhance your stay. Booking well in advance is advisable, particularly during peak festival seasons, to secure the best rates and availability.

Festival tickets and passes are essential components of your planning process. Many festivals offer a variety of ticketing options, from single-event tickets to all-access passes that grant entry to multiple performances and activities. Review the options available for each festival and select the one that best aligns with your interests and budget. Purchasing tickets in advance is often recommended, as popular events can sell out quickly. Additionally, be sure to check for any discounts or promotions that may be available, such as early-bird pricing or group rates.

As you prepare for your visit, take the time to familiarize yourself with the local culture and customs. Quebec is a province that prides itself on its distinct cultural identity, shaped by its French heritage and diverse influences. Learning a few basic phrases in French can enhance your interactions with locals and demonstrate your appreciation for the region's linguistic heritage. Additionally, understanding cultural norms and etiquette will help you navigate social situations with confidence and respect.

Packing for your festival adventure requires careful consideration of both the season and the specific events you'll be attending. If you're visiting during the winter months, be sure to pack warm clothing, including insulated jackets, hats, gloves, and waterproof boots, to stay comfortable in the cold. For summer festivals, lightweight clothing, sunscreen, and a reusable water bottle are essential for staying cool and hydrated. Regardless of the season, comfortable footwear is a must, as you'll likely spend a significant amount of time on your feet exploring festival grounds and venues.

As you embark on your festival journey, remain open to the unexpected and embrace the spontaneity that often accompanies such events. Festivals are dynamic, ever-evolving experiences that offer countless opportunities for discovery and connection. Be flexible in your plans and allow yourself the freedom to explore new interests and activities as they arise. Whether it's stumbling upon a hidden gem of a performance or striking up a conversation with fellow festival-goers, these serendipitous moments often become the most cherished memories of your visit.

Finally, consider incorporating downtime into your festival itinerary to recharge and reflect on your experiences. While it's tempting to fill every moment with activities and events, taking breaks allows you to fully appreciate the richness of the festival atmosphere and the beauty of your surroundings. Use this time to explore the local cuisine, visit nearby attractions, or simply relax and soak in the ambiance of Quebec's vibrant cities.

Navigating Quebec's festival calendar is an exhilarating endeavor that promises a wealth of unforgettable experiences. By planning thoughtfully and embracing the spontaneity of the festival spirit, you can create a memorable and enriching journey that celebrates the unique cultural tapestry of this remarkable province. As you immerse yourself in the sights and sounds of Quebec's festivals, you'll discover a world of creativity, diversity, and joy that transcends borders and brings people together in the shared celebration of life.

CHAPTER 5: EXPLORING NEIGHBORHOODS OF MONTREAL

Old Montreal: History Meets Modernity

Old Montreal stands as a testament to the rich tapestry of history and modernity woven into the very fabric of Quebec's largest city. Its cobblestone streets, lined with historic buildings and charming boutiques, transport visitors to a bygone era, while contemporary art galleries, chic cafes, and bustling markets breathe new life into this storied district. The juxtaposition of old and new creates a dynamic urban landscape, inviting exploration and discovery at every turn.

Wandering through Old Montreal, one is immediately struck by the architectural grandeur that defines the area. The district's buildings, many of which date back to the 17th and 18th centuries, showcase a blend of French and British influences, reflecting the city's colonial past. The iconic Notre-Dame Basilica, with its striking Gothic Revival façade and intricate interior, stands as a symbol of the city's spiritual and cultural heritage. Nearby, the Old Port offers a picturesque promenade along the St. Lawrence River, where the historic Clock Tower serves as a reminder of Montreal's maritime history.

Yet, Old Montreal is far from a mere relic of the past. In recent years, the district has undergone a renaissance, with a wave of revitalization projects breathing new life into its historic structures. Modern amenities and contemporary design elements have been seamlessly integrated into the area's historic fabric, creating a vibrant urban environment that appeals to both locals and visitors alike. This harmonious blend of old and new is perhaps best exemplified by the district's boutique hotels, where historic architecture meets modern luxury, offering guests a unique and immersive experience.

The culinary scene in Old Montreal is a testament to the district's dynamic character, offering a diverse array of dining options that cater to a wide range of tastes and preferences. From traditional French bistros serving classic dishes such as coq au vin and duck confit to contemporary fusion restaurants pushing the boundaries of gastronomy, the district is a food lover's paradise. Many establishments take advantage of the area's historic charm, with candle-lit dining rooms and outdoor terraces offering stunning views of the city's architectural landmarks.

For those seeking a taste of local flavor, the bustling Bonsecours Market is a must-visit destination. Housed in a historic domed building, the market is home to an eclectic mix of artisanal vendors, offering everything from gourmet cheeses and charcuterie to handmade crafts and souvenirs. This vibrant marketplace is a celebration of Quebec's rich culinary and artistic heritage, providing visitors with a unique opportunity to connect with local producers and artisans.

Art and culture are integral to the identity of Old Montreal, with a wealth of galleries, museums, and performance spaces offering a diverse array of creative experiences. The Montreal Museum of Archaeology and History, located at Pointe-à-Callière, provides a fascinating glimpse into the city's past, with exhibits that explore the area's indigenous heritage and colonial history. For contemporary art enthusiasts, the district's numerous galleries showcase the work of local and international artists, offering a window into the vibrant creativity that defines Montreal's cultural scene.

In the evenings, Old Montreal comes alive with a vibrant nightlife scene, offering a variety of options for those looking to unwind and enjoy the city's dynamic energy. Cozy wine bars and speakeasies offer intimate settings for conversation and relaxation, while lively pubs and clubs provide a more energetic atmosphere for dancing and socializing. The district's nightlife offerings cater to a wide range of tastes and preferences, ensuring that there is something for everyone to enjoy.

Despite its modern amenities and attractions, Old Montreal retains a sense of timelessness that is palpable to all who visit. The district's narrow streets and hidden alleyways invite exploration and discovery, offering glimpses into the city's storied past and the lives of those who have called it home. From the echoes of horse-drawn carriages on cobblestone streets to the distant tolling of church bells, Old Montreal is a place where history and modernity coexist in perfect harmony.

For those seeking a deeper connection to the city's past, guided walking tours offer an insightful journey through the history and architecture of Old Montreal. Led by knowledgeable guides, these tours provide a wealth of information about the district's landmarks and hidden gems, offering a unique perspective on the city's evolution over the centuries. Whether exploring on foot or by bicycle, visitors are encouraged to take their time and savor the rich tapestry of experiences that Old Montreal has to offer.

As the sun sets over the St. Lawrence River, casting a warm glow over the district's historic buildings, it becomes clear that Old Montreal is more than just a destination; it is an experience. It is a place where the past and present converge, creating a unique urban landscape that invites exploration and discovery. For those who visit, Old Montreal offers a glimpse into the heart and soul of a city that has embraced its history while looking boldly toward the future. Here, history meets modernity in a dance of contrasts, each complementing the other in a harmonious celebration of Montreal's enduring spirit.

Mile End: Hipster Vibes and Hidden Gems

Mile End, nestled in the heart of Montreal, is a vibrant neighborhood that exudes an eclectic mix of creativity, individuality, and charm. Known for its hipster vibes and hidden gems, this area has become a cultural hotspot, drawing artists, musicians, foodies, and curious explorers alike. With its bohemian spirit and rich tapestry of experiences, Mile End invites visitors to wander its streets and uncover the treasures that lie within.

A stroll through Mile End reveals a neighborhood that thrives on diversity and self-expression. The streets are lined with colorful murals and street art, each piece telling its own story and contributing to the area's unique character. This open-air gallery is a testament to the creativity that flourishes here, inviting passersby to pause and appreciate the artistry that adorns the urban landscape. It's a place where inspiration is never far away, and where every corner holds the promise of something unexpected.

The sense of community in Mile End is palpable, with a myriad of independent businesses that reflect the neighborhood's distinctive character. Quirky boutiques offer a curated selection of vintage clothing, handcrafted jewelry, and artisanal goods, catering to those with an eye for the unusual and the unique. These shops, often run by passionate locals, provide a personalized shopping experience that stands in stark contrast to the anonymity of large retail chains. It's a chance to discover one-of-a-kind treasures and support the artisans and entrepreneurs who call Mile End home.

The culinary scene in Mile End is a feast for the senses, offering a diverse array of flavors and cuisines that cater to every palate. From renowned bagel shops serving up freshly baked delights to cozy cafes offering expertly brewed coffee, the neighborhood is a haven for food lovers. The streets are dotted with eateries that celebrate global cuisine, from Middle Eastern falafel joints to Italian pizzerias and everything in between. These establishments, often characterized by their laid-back atmosphere and friendly service, invite visitors to savor the culinary diversity that defines Mile End.

Beyond its culinary offerings, Mile End is a hub for Montreal's burgeoning music and arts scene. Intimate venues and recording studios provide a platform for local musicians to showcase their talents, while art galleries display the work of emerging and established artists. The neighborhood's creative energy is further fueled by its numerous cultural events and festivals, which celebrate everything from music and film to literature and performance art. These gatherings foster a sense of camaraderie and collaboration, creating a vibrant community of artists and art enthusiasts.

For those seeking a more tranquil experience, Mile End's parks and green spaces offer a welcome respite from the urban hustle and bustle. Laurier Park, with its sprawling lawns and shaded pathways, is a popular spot for picnics, leisurely strolls, and outdoor activities. The park's serene atmosphere provides a perfect backdrop for relaxation and reflection, inviting visitors to unwind and enjoy the natural beauty of the surroundings. It's a reminder that amidst the neighborhood's dynamic energy, there is always a place to pause and recharge.

Mile End's unique charm lies in its ability to seamlessly blend the old with the new. Historic buildings and iconic landmarks stand alongside modern developments, creating a rich architectural tapestry that reflects the neighborhood's evolution over time. The Rialto Theatre, a stunning example of 1920s architecture, continues to captivate audiences with its diverse lineup of performances and events. Meanwhile, contemporary spaces like the Mile End Library offer a glimpse into the neighborhood's commitment to innovation and community engagement.

The people of Mile End are as diverse and dynamic as the neighborhood itself. A melting pot of cultures, backgrounds, and identities, the community is characterized by its openness and inclusivity. This sense of belonging is fostered by the neighborhood's many community initiatives and organizations, which work to support local residents and promote social cohesion. Whether through grassroots activism, cultural programming, or community events, the people of Mile End are united by their shared passion for their neighborhood and its future.

Exploring Mile End is a journey of discovery, where every visit offers new surprises and experiences. It's a place that invites curiosity and creativity, where the spirit of exploration is rewarded with hidden gems and unexpected delights. Whether you're a first-time visitor or a long-time resident, the neighborhood's ever-evolving landscape ensures that there is always something new to uncover and enjoy.

As the sun sets over Mile End, the neighborhood's vibrant energy continues to pulse through its streets. The sounds of live music spill out of venues, mingling with the laughter of friends gathered at cafes and bars. It's a place that never truly sleeps, where the spirit of creativity and community thrives long into the night. Mile End is more than just a neighborhood; it's a way of life—a celebration of individuality, diversity, and the joy of discovery.

In Mile End, the hipster vibes and hidden gems are not just part of the scenery; they are an integral part of the community's identity. It's a neighborhood that embraces its quirks and celebrates its uniqueness, inviting all who visit to do the same. Here, the ordinary becomes extraordinary, and the familiar transforms into something wonderfully new. Mile End is a testament to the power of creativity and the beauty of diversity, a place where everyone is welcome to explore, connect, and find their own hidden treasures.

Little Italy: A Culinary Destination

Little Italy in Montreal is a vibrant culinary destination that offers a rich tapestry of flavors, aromas, and experiences. This neighborhood is a treasure trove for food lovers, where the essence of Italian culture and cuisine comes alive in a lively and welcoming atmosphere. With its charming streets lined with cafes, restaurants, and specialty shops, Little Italy invites visitors on a gastronomic journey that delights the senses and warms the heart.

At the heart of Little Italy is the bustling Jean-Talon Market, one of the largest public markets in North America. This vibrant marketplace is a paradise for culinary enthusiasts, offering an array of fresh produce, meats, cheeses, and artisanal products. As you wander through the market, the colorful displays of fruits and vegetables capture your attention, while the enticing scents of freshly baked bread and pastries draw you in. Vendors proudly showcase their goods, inviting you to sample their offerings and share in their passion for quality and flavor. It's a place where the art of food is celebrated, and where every visit offers a new opportunity to discover and explore.

Beyond the market, Little Italy's streets are dotted with a variety of eateries that cater to every palate and preference. Traditional trattorias serve up classic Italian dishes, from hearty pasta and risotto to succulent osso buco and tender veal scaloppine. These family-run establishments often feature recipes passed down through generations, offering an authentic taste of Italy that transports diners to the heart of the Mediterranean. The warm and inviting ambiance of these restaurants, coupled with the genuine hospitality of their hosts, creates a dining experience that is both comforting and memorable.

For those seeking more contemporary fare, Little Italy is home to a number of modern Italian restaurants that blend tradition with innovation. These establishments offer creative takes on classic dishes, incorporating fresh, local ingredients and modern cooking techniques to create a unique culinary experience. Whether it's a wood-fired pizza topped with seasonal vegetables or a delicate seafood risotto infused with aromatic herbs, these dishes are a testament to the neighborhood's dynamic and evolving food scene.

Little Italy's cafes and bakeries are a haven for those with a sweet tooth, offering an array of delectable pastries, gelato, and desserts. The scent of freshly brewed espresso wafts through the air, inviting visitors to pause and savor a moment of indulgence. From flaky sfogliatelle and creamy cannoli to rich tiramisu and velvety panna cotta, these sweet treats are a celebration of Italian culinary artistry. Enjoying a coffee and pastry at a sidewalk cafe is a quintessential Little Italy experience, offering a chance to relax and soak in the vibrant atmosphere.

In addition to its culinary delights, Little Italy is a neighborhood rich in history and culture. The area is home to beautiful churches, cultural institutions, and community centers that reflect the deep-rooted traditions and heritage of its residents. The Church of the Madonna della Difesa, with its stunning frescoes and intricate architecture, stands as a testament to the neighborhood's strong Italian Catholic roots. Meanwhile, cultural events and festivals, such as the Italian Week Montreal, celebrate the vibrant spirit and contributions of the Italian community, offering a glimpse into the customs and traditions that have shaped the neighborhood.

The sense of community in Little Italy is palpable, with residents and visitors alike coming together to celebrate their shared love of food and culture. This is a neighborhood where relationships are forged over a shared meal, where stories are exchanged and laughter fills the air. It's a place where the warmth of Italian hospitality is extended to all who visit, creating a sense of belonging and connection that transcends borders.

For those looking to bring a taste of Little Italy home, the neighborhood's specialty shops offer an array of gourmet products and ingredients. From imported olive oils and balsamic vinegars to artisanal pasta and cheeses, these stores provide everything needed to recreate the flavors of Italy in your own kitchen. The knowledgeable shopkeepers are always eager to share their expertise, offering tips and recommendations to help you craft the perfect Italian meal.

Exploring Little Italy is a journey of discovery, where each visit offers new tastes, experiences, and memories. It's a neighborhood that invites you to slow down, savor each moment, and appreciate the simple pleasures of life. Whether you're enjoying a leisurely meal with friends, sampling the vibrant flavors of the market, or wandering the charming streets, Little Italy captures the essence of la dolce vita—the sweet life.

As the sun sets and the neighborhood comes alive with the sounds of conversation and laughter, it's clear that Little Italy is more than just a culinary destination. It's a celebration of culture, community, and the joy of sharing a meal with loved ones. In Little Italy, food is not just sustenance; it's an expression of love and tradition, a way of bringing people together and creating lasting connections. Here, the spirit of Italy is alive and well, offering a taste of the old world in the heart of Montreal.

The Gay Village: Vibrant Culture and Nightlife

The Gay Village in Montreal stands as a beacon of diversity, inclusion, and vibrant energy, drawing people from all walks of life to experience its dynamic culture and thriving nightlife. As one of the largest gay neighborhoods in North America, it offers a sanctuary where individuality is celebrated and the spirit of community thrives. With its colorful streets, eclectic venues, and welcoming atmosphere, the Village is a testament to Montreal's commitment to embracing diversity and fostering a sense of belonging.

Stepping into the Gay Village, one is immediately enveloped in a vibrant tapestry of sights and sounds. The main thoroughfare, Sainte-Catherine Street, is transformed into a pedestrian-only zone during the warmer months, allowing visitors to leisurely explore the array of attractions the neighborhood has to offer. Above, the iconic rainbow-colored canopy of art installations stretches across the length of the street, casting a kaleidoscope of colors onto the bustling scene below. This visual celebration of pride and unity serves as a powerful reminder of the progress made towards equality and acceptance.

The cultural richness of the Gay Village is reflected in its diverse array of establishments, each offering a unique experience that caters to a wide range of interests and tastes.

Art enthusiasts can explore the many galleries and exhibition spaces that showcase the work of local and international artists, providing a platform for creative expression and dialogue. The neighborhood's theaters and performance venues host a variety of shows, from cutting-edge contemporary productions to classic revivals, ensuring there is always something to captivate and inspire.

For those with a passion for culinary exploration, the Gay Village is home to an eclectic mix of restaurants, cafes, and eateries that celebrate flavors from around the world. From trendy bistros serving up innovative dishes to cozy diners offering comfort food classics, the neighborhood's dining scene is as diverse as its community. Many establishments feature outdoor terraces, inviting patrons to enjoy their meals while soaking in the lively atmosphere that defines the Village. Whether you're savoring a leisurely brunch or indulging in a late-night snack, the culinary offerings are sure to delight and satisfy.

As the sun sets, the Gay Village comes alive with a vibrant nightlife scene that is both inclusive and exhilarating. The neighborhood boasts a plethora of bars, clubs, and lounges, each offering its own unique ambiance and entertainment. From laid-back pubs where patrons can enjoy a quiet drink to high-energy dance clubs that pulsate with music and excitement, the nightlife options cater to every mood and preference. Many venues host themed nights, drag shows, and live performances, ensuring that there is always something new and exciting to experience.

One of the defining features of the Gay Village's nightlife is its sense of inclusivity and acceptance. Here, people of all identities and orientations are welcomed with open arms, creating a safe and supportive environment where everyone is free to express themselves without judgment. This spirit of camaraderie and celebration permeates the neighborhood, fostering a sense of unity and belonging that is palpable to all who visit.

Beyond its entertainment offerings, the Gay Village is also a hub for activism and advocacy, playing a vital role in advancing LGBTQ+ rights and visibility. The neighborhood is home to a number of organizations and community centers that provide support, resources, and outreach to individuals in need. These organizations work tirelessly to promote equality, raise awareness, and effect positive change, ensuring that the Village remains a beacon of hope and progress for the LGBTQ+ community.

The annual Pride Festival is a highlight of the Gay Village's cultural calendar, drawing thousands of visitors from around the world to celebrate love, diversity, and acceptance. This multi-day event features a vibrant parade, live performances, and a host of activities that showcase the creativity and resilience of the LGBTQ+ community. The festival is a joyous celebration of identity and pride, offering an opportunity for individuals to come together and honor the strides made towards equality while recognizing the work that remains to be done.

Exploring the Gay Village is a journey of discovery, where every visit offers new experiences and connections. It's a neighborhood that invites you to embrace your true self, celebrate your individuality, and engage with a community that champions diversity and inclusion. Whether you're immersing yourself in the arts, savoring the culinary delights, or dancing the night away, the Village offers a welcoming and vibrant space where everyone is free to be themselves.

As dawn breaks and the city awakens, the Gay Village remains a symbol of resilience and hope, a reminder of the power of community and the importance of standing together in the face of adversity. It is a place where the spirit of love and acceptance is alive and well, offering a sanctuary for those seeking connection and belonging. In the Gay Village, vibrant culture and nightlife converge to create a dynamic and enduring celebration of life, love, and the pursuit of equality. Here, the journey towards a more inclusive future continues, one step, one dance, one moment at a time.

Saint-Henri: Industrial Past, Artistic Present

Saint-Henri, a neighborhood in Montreal with an industrial past, has undergone a remarkable transformation into a vibrant artistic hub. This district, once known for its factories and working-class roots, now thrives as a center of creativity and innovation, drawing artists, musicians, and artisans who infuse the area with new life and energy. The juxtaposition of its historical legacy with contemporary artistic endeavors creates a dynamic environment where the old and the new coexist in harmony.

The roots of Saint-Henri's industrial history are still visible in its architecture, with brick warehouses and factories standing as enduring symbols of the neighborhood's past. These structures, once bustling with the activity of manufacturing and production, have been repurposed into lofts, studios, and galleries that now serve as creative spaces for artists and entrepreneurs. This adaptive reuse of industrial buildings not only preserves the architectural heritage of the area but also provides a unique backdrop for artistic expression and innovation. The high ceilings, open spaces, and raw materials of these buildings offer artists the freedom to experiment and create, fostering an environment of boundless creativity.

Walking through the streets of Saint-Henri, one can feel the pulse of artistic energy that permeates the neighborhood. Murals and street art adorn the walls, transforming the urban landscape into an open-air gallery that celebrates the diversity and talent of local artists. These vibrant works of art not only beautify the area but also spark conversation and reflection, inviting residents and visitors alike to engage with the creative spirit of the community. The neighborhood's commitment to public art initiatives further cements its reputation as a haven for artistic expression and cultural dialogue.

Saint-Henri's artistic renaissance is fueled by a thriving community of creators who call the neighborhood home. Art galleries and studios showcase a wide range of disciplines, from painting and sculpture to photography and mixed media. These spaces provide a platform for emerging and established artists to share their work with the public, fostering a sense of connection and collaboration within the community. Regular exhibitions and open studio events invite art enthusiasts to explore the diverse talents of Saint-Henri's creative residents, offering a glimpse into the vibrant world of contemporary art.

The neighborhood's cultural evolution is also reflected in its lively music scene, which draws performers and audiences from across the city. Small venues and intimate performance spaces host live music events that range from indie rock and jazz to electronic and experimental sounds. These gatherings create a sense of camaraderie and shared experience, as music lovers come together to celebrate the diverse sounds and rhythms that define Saint-Henri's musical landscape. The presence of recording studios and rehearsal spaces further supports the neighborhood's musical community, providing artists with the resources they need to hone their craft and share their talents with the world.

In addition to its artistic offerings, Saint-Henri boasts a culinary scene that reflects the neighborhood's eclectic character and cultural diversity. From cozy cafes and artisanal bakeries to innovative restaurants and bustling food markets, the area offers a wealth of dining options that cater to a wide range of tastes and preferences. Many establishments take advantage of the neighborhood's industrial architecture, with stylish interiors that blend rustic charm with contemporary design. Whether savoring a freshly brewed coffee or indulging in a gourmet meal, visitors to Saint-Henri are treated to a culinary experience that is as creative and diverse as the neighborhood itself.

The sense of community in Saint-Henri is palpable, with residents and visitors alike coming together to participate in cultural events, workshops, and festivals that celebrate the neighborhood's artistic spirit. These gatherings foster a sense of belonging and connection, creating opportunities for collaboration and dialogue among artists, creators, and enthusiasts. Whether through art walks, pop-up markets, or live performances, the neighborhood's cultural calendar is filled with events that invite participation and engagement, enriching the lives of those who live and visit here.

Despite its transformation, Saint-Henri remains deeply connected to its industrial roots, with a history that continues to shape its identity and character. The neighborhood's evolution from an industrial hub to an artistic haven is a testament to the resilience and adaptability of its community, as well as the power of creativity to inspire change and renewal. By embracing its past while looking toward the future, Saint-Henri has carved out a unique niche within Montreal's cultural landscape, offering a model for other neighborhoods seeking to balance heritage with innovation.

Exploring Saint-Henri is a journey through time and creativity, where the echoes of the past resonate in harmony with the vibrant expressions of the present. It's a place that invites curiosity and exploration, where every street corner and alleyway holds the promise of discovery. Whether you're admiring the architectural beauty of a repurposed factory, enjoying the sounds of a live performance, or engaging with the work of a local artist, Saint-Henri offers a rich tapestry of experiences that celebrate the intersection of industry and art.

As the sun sets over the neighborhood, casting a warm glow on its historic buildings and bustling streets, it becomes clear that Saint-Henri is more than just a destination; it's a living, breathing community that embodies the spirit of creativity and innovation. Here, the industrial past meets the artistic present in a harmonious dance that celebrates the resilience and ingenuity of its people. In Saint-Henri, the story of transformation and renewal continues to unfold, offering inspiration and hope for the future.

Westmount: Elegant Mansions and Green Spaces

Westmount, a distinguished enclave in Montreal, exudes an air of elegance and tranquility, characterized by its stately mansions and lush green spaces. This affluent neighborhood, nestled on the slopes of Mount Royal, offers a serene escape from the bustling city while maintaining close proximity to urban amenities. With its tree-lined streets, historic architecture, and meticulously maintained parks, Westmount represents a harmonious blend of sophistication and natural beauty.

The architecture of Westmount is a testament to the neighborhood's rich history and refined taste. Grand mansions and heritage homes, many dating back to the late 19th and early 20th centuries, line the avenues, each with its own unique charm and character. These residences, often designed in styles ranging from Victorian and Edwardian to Tudor and Neo-Gothic, showcase the craftsmanship and attention to detail that define the area's architectural heritage. Intricate stonework, ornate wood detailing, and expansive gardens are hallmarks of these elegant homes, offering a glimpse into the opulent lifestyles of their original inhabitants.

While Westmount's architectural beauty is undeniable, the neighborhood's commitment to preserving its natural surroundings is equally impressive. Westmount Park, a sprawling oasis in the heart of the community, provides a verdant retreat for residents and visitors alike. The park's meticulously landscaped grounds feature walking paths, ponds, and gardens, inviting leisurely strolls and moments of reflection amidst nature's splendor. The scent of blooming flowers and the gentle rustle of leaves create a soothing ambiance, offering a welcome respite from the urban hustle and bustle.

In addition to Westmount Park, the neighborhood boasts a number of smaller parks and green spaces that cater to a variety of recreational activities. Murray Hill Park, with its panoramic views of the city and Mount Royal, is a popular destination for picnics and outdoor gatherings. The park's expansive lawns and wooded areas provide ample space for children to play and adults to relax, fostering a sense of community and connection among residents. Meanwhile, Summit Woods and Summit Circle offer a more rugged landscape, with hiking trails and lookout points that reward visitors with breathtaking vistas of the city below.

Westmount's commitment to education and cultural enrichment is evident in its numerous institutions and facilities that cater to a wide range of interests and pursuits. The Westmount Public Library, housed in a historic building with stunning architectural details, serves as a hub for literary and intellectual engagement. The library offers a diverse collection of books, periodicals, and digital resources, as well as a variety of programs and events that cater to readers of all ages. This beloved institution is a testament to the neighborhood's dedication to fostering lifelong learning and community engagement.

For those with an appreciation for the arts, the Westmount area is home to several galleries and cultural centers that showcase the work of local and international artists. These spaces provide a platform for creative expression and cultural dialogue, enriching the community with a diverse array of visual and performing arts experiences. From gallery exhibitions and art workshops to theater performances and musical concerts, Westmount offers a wealth of opportunities for residents and visitors to engage with the arts and connect with one another.

Westmount's vibrant community spirit is further reflected in its array of clubs, associations, and organizations that cater to a wide range of interests and activities. From gardening clubs and historical societies to sports teams and charitable organizations, these groups foster a sense of camaraderie and collaboration among residents. Community events, such as seasonal festivals, art fairs, and charity fundraisers, bring people together to celebrate and support one another, strengthening the bonds that define this close-knit neighborhood.

The neighborhood's commercial district, centered around Sherbrooke Street and Greene Avenue, offers a curated selection of boutiques, cafes, and specialty shops that cater to discerning tastes. These establishments, often run by local entrepreneurs, provide a personalized shopping and dining experience that reflects the refined character of Westmount. From high-end fashion and artisanal goods to gourmet cuisine and fine wines, the neighborhood's offerings are as diverse as they are sophisticated, ensuring that residents and visitors alike have access to the finest in quality and service.

Despite its reputation for elegance and exclusivity, Westmount is a welcoming and inclusive community that values diversity and connection. The neighborhood's residents, drawn from a wide range of backgrounds and professions, share a common appreciation for the area's beauty and tranquility, as well as a commitment to preserving its unique character and charm. This sense of shared purpose and pride fosters a strong sense of community, where neighbors come together to support and celebrate one another.

Exploring Westmount is an invitation to experience the finer things in life, from the grandeur of its historic mansions to the serenity of its green spaces. It's a place where beauty and elegance are celebrated, and where the past and present coexist in perfect harmony. Whether you're admiring the architectural splendor of a heritage home, savoring a leisurely afternoon in a park, or engaging with the cultural and intellectual offerings of the community, Westmount offers a rich tapestry of experiences that delight and inspire.

As the sun sets over the neighborhood, casting a warm glow on its stately homes and verdant landscapes, it becomes clear that Westmount is more than just a place to live; it's a way of life. Here, elegance and tranquility are not mere luxuries, but essential elements of a community that values beauty, harmony, and connection. In Westmount, the pursuit of excellence and the appreciation of nature go hand in hand, creating a neighborhood that is as timeless as it is inviting.

Verdun: Riverside Strolls and Local Eats

Verdun, a charming neighborhood nestled along the banks of the Saint Lawrence River, offers an inviting blend of natural beauty and culinary delights. This vibrant community, known for its scenic riverside paths and burgeoning food scene, provides a serene yet dynamic environment for both residents and visitors. Verdun's appeal lies in its ability to harmoniously combine leisurely outdoor experiences with the thrill of discovering local culinary treasures, making it a must-visit destination for those seeking a taste of Montreal's diverse offerings.

The riverside paths of Verdun are a defining feature of the neighborhood, offering picturesque views and a tranquil escape from the city's hustle and bustle. These paths, part of the larger network of green spaces that line the Saint Lawrence River, invite leisurely strolls, invigorating jogs, and peaceful bike rides. As you wander along the water's edge, the gentle lapping of the river and the rustling of leaves create a soothing soundtrack, enhancing the sense of peace and relaxation that Verdun provides.

The Verdun waterfront also offers a connection to nature that is rare within urban environments. Parks like Parc de l'Honorable-George-O'Reilly and Parc Arthur-Therrien provide ample green space for picnics, family gatherings, and outdoor activities. The lush lawns and shaded benches create a welcoming atmosphere for those looking to unwind, while playgrounds and sports facilities cater to the neighborhood's more active visitors. From yoga sessions by the river to community events and festivals, Verdun's green spaces are alive with activity and a testament to the neighborhood's vibrant community spirit.

A standout feature of Verdun's riverside experience is its accessibility to water sports and recreational activities. The neighborhood's proximity to the river makes it an ideal location for kayaking, paddleboarding, and canoeing, offering adventure-seekers the opportunity to explore the waterways and take in the stunning views from a different perspective. Verdun's local outfitters and rental shops provide the necessary equipment and guidance, ensuring that both novices and experienced paddlers can enjoy the river's offerings safely and confidently.

Complementing Verdun's natural attractions is its diverse and thriving culinary scene, which reflects the neighborhood's cultural richness and creativity. From cozy cafes and bustling bistros to innovative restaurants and artisanal bakeries, Verdun's dining establishments offer a wide array of flavors and experiences that cater to every palate and preference. The neighborhood's culinary entrepreneurs are known for their commitment to quality and sustainability, often sourcing ingredients from local producers and suppliers to create dishes that highlight the best of what the region has to offer.

One of Verdun's culinary highlights is its vibrant café culture, where patrons can enjoy expertly brewed coffee and freshly baked pastries in a relaxed and inviting setting. These cafes, often featuring locally roasted beans and artisanal treats, provide the perfect spot to catch up with friends, read a book, or simply savor a quiet moment of indulgence. With their warm ambiance and friendly staff, Verdun's cafes embody the neighborhood's welcoming spirit and dedication to fostering connections within the community.

For those seeking a more substantial meal, Verdun's restaurants offer a diverse range of cuisines and dining experiences, from casual eateries to upscale dining establishments. Whether you're in the mood for hearty comfort food, international flavors, or innovative plant-based dishes, the neighborhood's chefs and restaurateurs are sure to satisfy your culinary cravings. Many of these establishments take pride in showcasing local ingredients and seasonal produce, offering menus that are both creative and rooted in the region's culinary traditions.

Verdun is also home to a number of specialty food shops and markets, where food enthusiasts can discover unique ingredients and gourmet products. These establishments offer everything from artisanal cheeses and charcuterie to freshly baked bread and handcrafted sweets, providing the perfect opportunity to explore new flavors and support local producers. The knowledgeable shopkeepers are always eager to share their expertise and recommendations, helping you find the perfect addition to your next meal or gathering.

The neighborhood's commitment to community and sustainability is evident in its support for local food initiatives and urban agriculture projects. Verdun's community gardens and farmers' markets provide residents with access to fresh, locally grown produce, while promoting environmentally friendly practices and fostering a sense of connection to the land. These initiatives not only contribute to the neighborhood's culinary offerings but also strengthen the bonds between residents and create a shared sense of purpose and responsibility.

Verdun's blend of riverside strolls and local eats offers a unique and enriching experience for those seeking a taste of Montreal's natural beauty and culinary diversity. The neighborhood's welcoming atmosphere, combined with its commitment to quality and sustainability, makes it a destination that invites exploration and discovery. Whether you're enjoying a leisurely walk along the river, indulging in a delicious meal, or browsing the offerings of a local market, Verdun provides a rich tapestry of experiences that celebrate the best of what the city has to offer.

As the sun sets over the Saint Lawrence River, casting a warm glow on the water and the streets of Verdun, it becomes clear that this neighborhood is more than just a destination; it's a vibrant community that values connection, creativity, and the simple pleasures of life. Verdun's riverside paths and culinary delights offer a harmonious blend of relaxation and excitement, creating a place where residents and visitors alike can savor the beauty and richness of Montreal's diverse landscape. Here, the journey is as rewarding as the destination, inviting you to slow down, explore, and enjoy all that Verdun has to offer.

CHAPTER 6: EXPLORING NEIGHBORHOODS OF QUEBEC CITY

Old Quebec: The Heart of French-Canadian Culture

Old Quebec, a UNESCO World Heritage site, stands as a vibrant testament to the enduring spirit of French-Canadian culture. Nestled within the walls of Quebec City, this historic district embodies the rich tapestry of history, architecture, and tradition that defines the province. With its cobblestone streets, centuries-old buildings, and lively atmosphere, Old Quebec offers a glimpse into a bygone era while remaining a dynamic and thriving cultural hub.

The heart of Old Quebec is its architecture, a blend of French, British, and North American influences that tells the story of the city's evolution over the centuries. The iconic Château Frontenac, a grand hotel that dominates the skyline, serves as a symbol of the area's historical significance and architectural grandeur. Its turrets and towers, reminiscent of a fairy tale castle, offer panoramic views of the St. Lawrence River and the surrounding cityscape. This majestic structure, along with the stately fortifications that encircle the district, provides a tangible connection to the past, inviting visitors to step back in time and explore the rich history that shaped this region.

Wandering through the narrow streets of Old Quebec, one encounters a wealth of historic sites and landmarks that offer insight into the city's storied past. The Notre-Dame de Québec Basilica-Cathedral, with its stunning façade and intricate interior, stands as a testament to the enduring influence of the Catholic Church in the region. As the oldest parish in North America, it holds a special place in the hearts of Quebecers, serving as a spiritual and cultural center for the community.

Nearby, the Place Royale, often referred to as the birthplace of French America, is a charming square that transports visitors to the early days of the colony, with its cobbled streets and preserved 17th-century buildings.

In addition to its architectural treasures, Old Quebec is home to a vibrant cultural scene that celebrates the unique heritage and traditions of the region. The district hosts a variety of festivals and events throughout the year, each offering a unique opportunity to experience the music, dance, and cuisine that define French-Canadian culture. The Winter Carnival, with its ice sculptures, parades, and outdoor activities, is a highlight of the calendar, drawing visitors from around the world to celebrate the joys of the season. Similarly, the New France Festival, held each summer, brings the history of the colony to life with period costumes, historical reenactments, and culinary delights.

Old Quebec's culinary scene is a reflection of its cultural diversity and rich history, offering a range of flavors and experiences that cater to every palate. From quaint bistros serving traditional French fare to modern eateries that fuse local ingredients with international influences, the district's dining establishments showcase the creativity and passion of Quebec's chefs. The emphasis on fresh, locally sourced produce is evident in every dish, whether it's a classic tourtière, a savory poutine, or a delicate tarte au sucre. For those seeking a taste of the region's renowned artisanal products, the local markets offer an array of cheeses, charcuterie, and maple delicacies that are sure to satisfy even the most discerning gourmand.

Beyond its culinary offerings, Old Quebec is a haven for art and culture enthusiasts, with a wealth of galleries, museums, and performance spaces that highlight the creativity and talent of the region's artists. The Musée de l'Amérique francophone, housed in a historic building that was once a seminary, provides a fascinating exploration of the history and heritage of French America. Its exhibitions, which range from historical artifacts to contemporary art, offer a comprehensive look at the cultural influences that have shaped the region. Meanwhile, the Quartier Petit Champlain, one of the oldest shopping districts in North America, is a charming area filled with boutiques, artisan shops, and galleries that showcase the work of local creators.

Old Quebec's commitment to preserving its cultural heritage is evident in its dedication to education and community engagement. The district is home to a number of educational institutions and cultural organizations that provide resources and support for those seeking to learn about and celebrate the region's unique history and traditions. Workshops, lectures, and guided tours offer opportunities for residents and visitors alike to deepen their understanding of French-Canadian culture and to connect with the stories and experiences that have shaped the community.

As the sun sets over Old Quebec, casting a golden glow on the historic buildings and bustling streets, the district comes alive with the sounds of street performers, musicians, and laughter. The lively atmosphere, combined with the area's rich history and cultural offerings, creates a sense of enchantment and wonder that captivates all who visit. Whether you're exploring the winding streets, savoring a delicious meal, or engaging with the vibrant arts scene, Old Quebec offers a truly immersive experience that celebrates the heart and soul of French-Canadian culture.

In Old Quebec, the past and present converge to create a dynamic and living tapestry that is both timeless and ever-evolving. The district's commitment to preserving its unique heritage, while embracing new ideas and influences, ensures that it remains a vital and thriving cultural hub for generations to come. Here, the spirit of French-Canadian culture is alive and well, offering a warm welcome to all who seek to explore and celebrate the rich history and vibrant traditions that define this remarkable region.

Saint-Roch: Trendy Bars and Art Galleries

Saint-Roch, a vibrant neighborhood in Quebec City, has transformed into a bustling district renowned for its trendy bars and art galleries. Once an industrial area, Saint-Roch has experienced a cultural renaissance, drawing artists, entrepreneurs, and creatives who have infused it with new energy and innovation. This revitalization has turned the neighborhood into a dynamic hub where the allure of nightlife and the charm of visual arts coexist harmoniously.

The streets of Saint-Roch pulse with excitement, offering a rich tapestry of experiences for those who venture into its lively embrace. At the heart of this neighborhood's appeal are its trendy bars, each offering unique atmospheres and eclectic menus that cater to a diverse clientele. From craft cocktails to locally brewed beers, the bars of Saint-Roch provide an extensive array of libations for every taste. Whether you're seeking a refined speakeasy ambiance or a lively pub atmosphere, the neighborhood's establishments offer a convivial environment that encourages socializing and connection.

The bartenders of Saint-Roch are artisans in their own right, crafting drinks with a level of precision and creativity that elevates the cocktail experience to an art form. Their passion for mixology is evident in the innovative concoctions they create, often featuring locally sourced ingredients and house-made infusions. These skilled professionals are always eager to share their expertise, guiding patrons through the intricacies of their craft and offering recommendations tailored to individual preferences. In Saint-Roch, the act of enjoying a drink becomes a sensory journey, where flavors and aromas intertwine to create memorable experiences.

Complementing the vibrant bar scene is Saint-Roch's thriving art community, which has established the neighborhood as a cultural hotspot. A stroll through the streets reveals a plethora of art galleries, each showcasing an impressive array of works by local and international artists. These galleries, often housed in repurposed industrial spaces, provide a platform for emerging and established artists to display their creations, offering visitors an opportunity to engage with a diverse spectrum of styles and mediums. Paintings, sculptures, photographs, and installations adorn the walls, inviting contemplation and sparking dialogue among art enthusiasts.

The art galleries of Saint-Roch are more than just exhibition spaces; they are integral to the neighborhood's identity and cultural vitality. Regular gallery openings, artist talks, and workshops foster a sense of community and collaboration, bringing together artists, collectors, and appreciators of the arts. These events create opportunities for meaningful exchanges, where ideas are shared, and connections are forged. The galleries serve as incubators for creativity, nurturing the talents of artists and contributing to the cultural landscape of the city.

Beyond its bars and galleries, Saint-Roch is a vibrant neighborhood that embraces diversity and innovation. The area's revitalization has attracted a variety of businesses and entrepreneurs, from boutique shops and cafes to tech start-ups and co-working spaces. This eclectic mix of enterprises reflects the neighborhood's dynamic character and its openness to new ideas and ventures. The entrepreneurial spirit that permeates Saint-Roch is a testament to its resilience and adaptability, qualities that have fueled its transformation into a thriving urban community.

The neighborhood's culinary scene is equally diverse, offering a range of dining options that cater to both traditional and adventurous palates. Restaurants in Saint-Roch pride themselves on their inventive menus and commitment to quality, often highlighting locally sourced ingredients and sustainable practices. From gourmet dining experiences to casual eateries, the culinary offerings in Saint-Roch are as varied as they are delicious, ensuring that every meal is a celebration of flavor and creativity.

Saint-Roch's public spaces further enhance its appeal, providing residents and visitors with areas to relax, socialize, and enjoy the neighborhood's unique ambiance. Parks, plazas, and green spaces are thoughtfully integrated into the urban landscape, offering a respite from the bustling streets and a place for community gatherings. These spaces are often animated by street performers, musicians, and artists, adding to the neighborhood's vibrant atmosphere and sense of community.

The transformation of Saint-Roch into a trendy, cultural hub is a testament to the power of creativity and collaboration in revitalizing urban spaces. The neighborhood's evolution from an industrial area to a thriving district of bars, galleries, and innovative enterprises highlights the potential for growth and renewal in urban environments. The spirit of Saint-Roch lies in its ability to embrace change while preserving its unique character and charm, creating a community that is as welcoming as it is dynamic.

As you explore Saint-Roch, the neighborhood unfolds as a rich tapestry of experiences, where the energy of nightlife and the allure of art come together to create a vibrant and engaging environment. Whether you're savoring a meticulously crafted cocktail, admiring a thought-provoking piece of art, or simply enjoying the lively streetscape, Saint-Roch offers a unique blend of urban vitality and cultural richness. Here, the past and present converge, shaping a neighborhood that continues to inspire and captivate all who visit.

Montcalm: Museums and Quiet Streets

Montcalm, a tranquil and culturally rich neighborhood in Quebec City, offers a unique blend of serene residential streets and vibrant artistic venues. Known for its quiet charm and intellectual allure, Montcalm is a haven for those seeking an immersive cultural experience centered around its esteemed museums and the peaceful ambiance of its tree-lined avenues. This neighborhood, with its understated elegance, invites both locals and visitors to explore the depth of its historical and artistic offerings.

The museums of Montcalm stand as pillars of the neighborhood's cultural identity, offering diverse collections that span art, history, and science. Among these, the Musée national des beaux-arts du Québec (MNBAQ) is a crowning jewel, housing an extensive collection of Quebecois art that spans several centuries. This museum, set within the picturesque Plains of Abraham, features a harmonious blend of historic and contemporary architecture, with its various pavilions interconnected through thoughtfully designed spaces. As you wander through its galleries, the evolution of Quebec's artistic landscape unfolds before you, with works ranging from traditional landscapes and portraits to contemporary installations and multimedia creations.

The MNBAQ's commitment to showcasing local talent is evident in its rotating exhibitions, which highlight the contributions of emerging and established artists from the region. These exhibitions provide a platform for artistic innovation and dialogue, encouraging visitors to engage with the works on display and consider the cultural and social contexts from which they emerge. The museum's programming, which includes artist talks, workshops, and educational initiatives, further enriches the visitor experience, offering opportunities for deeper engagement and learning.

Beyond the MNBAQ, Montcalm is home to several other cultural institutions that contribute to its reputation as a hub for intellectual and artistic exploration. The neighborhood's smaller galleries and cultural centers offer intimate settings for discovering new artists and appreciating diverse forms of expression. These spaces, often tucked away on quiet side streets, provide a contrast to the grandeur of larger museums, inviting visitors to engage with art in a more personal and contemplative manner. The exhibitions held in these venues often reflect the neighborhood's eclectic character, showcasing a wide range of styles and mediums that capture the essence of contemporary creativity.

The quiet streets of Montcalm provide a serene backdrop to the neighborhood's cultural offerings, inviting leisurely strolls and moments of reflection. As you wander through the area, the architecture speaks to the history and evolution of the city, with its mix of elegant townhouses, charming cottages, and modern residences. The meticulous landscaping and well-preserved facades reflect the pride of Montcalm's residents in maintaining the neighborhood's heritage and character. The sense of tranquility that pervades the streets is enhanced by the presence of mature trees and lush gardens, creating an oasis of calm within the urban landscape.

Montcalm's cafes and bistros contribute to the neighborhood's inviting atmosphere, offering cozy retreats where patrons can enjoy a leisurely coffee or a delicious meal. These establishments, often family-owned and operated, emphasize quality and authenticity, with menus that feature locally sourced ingredients and traditional recipes. The cafes, with their warm interiors and friendly staff, provide the perfect setting for relaxed conversations or quiet moments of introspection, embodying the neighborhood's spirit of hospitality and community.

For those seeking a deeper connection to Montcalm's cultural offerings, the neighborhood's educational institutions and community organizations play an integral role in fostering a sense of engagement and belonging. These entities offer a variety of programs and events that cater to diverse interests, from art classes and literary workshops to lectures and panel discussions. By providing opportunities for learning and collaboration, these organizations strengthen the bonds within the community and encourage residents and visitors alike to participate in the cultural life of the neighborhood.

Montcalm's commitment to preserving its cultural and historical heritage is evident in its dedication to sustainable urban development and green initiatives. The neighborhood's parks and public spaces are thoughtfully designed to promote environmental stewardship and enhance the quality of life for residents. The Plains of Abraham, with its expansive lawns and scenic vistas, offers a natural retreat for those seeking respite from the city's bustle. This historic site, with its rich history and cultural significance, serves as a gathering place for community events and recreational activities, fostering a sense of connection to the land and its stories.

Montcalm's appeal lies in its ability to offer a harmonious blend of cultural richness and tranquil living, creating an environment where residents and visitors can enjoy the best of both worlds. The neighborhood's museums and quiet streets provide a canvas for exploration and reflection, inviting those who wander its paths to engage with the art, history, and natural beauty that define this unique corner of Quebec City.

As the sun sets over Montcalm, casting a warm glow on its leafy streets and historic facades, the neighborhood's charm becomes even more apparent. The gentle rustle of leaves and the soft murmur of conversation create a soothing ambiance, inviting residents and visitors to savor the tranquility and cultural richness that Montcalm has to offer. Whether you're exploring a museum, enjoying a quiet walk, or savoring a meal at a local bistro, Montcalm offers a unique and enriching experience that celebrates the art of living well. Here, in this quiet enclave, the beauty of the present is enhanced by a deep appreciation for the past, creating a neighborhood that is as timeless as it is inviting.

Saint-Jean-Baptiste: The Bohemian District

Saint-Jean-Baptiste, often referred to as the Bohemian District, exudes a distinct charm that sets it apart from other neighborhoods in Quebec City. This eclectic area, with its vibrant arts scene and alternative spirit, serves as a haven for creatives, free thinkers, and those seeking a unique and authentic experience. The district's lively streets, adorned with colorful murals and quirky boutiques, invite exploration and discovery, offering a sensory feast that captivates all who wander its paths.

The essence of Saint-Jean-Baptiste lies in its bohemian soul, a spirit that embraces individuality and celebrates diversity. This neighborhood, with its mix of historic architecture and contemporary influences, creates an environment where creativity flourishes. The streets are lined with independent shops and studios, each offering a glimpse into the district's artistic heart. From vintage clothing stores to artisanal craft shops, the entrepreneurial spirit of Saint-Jean-Baptiste is evident, showcasing the talents and passions of its residents.

Artistic expression is woven into the fabric of Saint-Jean-Baptiste, with street art playing a central role in the neighborhood's identity. Murals and graffiti adorn the walls of buildings, transforming them into canvases that tell stories and spark conversation. These vibrant works of art are not only visually striking but also serve as a reflection of the community's values and aspirations. They capture the essence of the neighborhood's rebellious and forward-thinking spirit, inviting passersby to pause and engage with the messages conveyed through color and form.

The heart of the district's bohemian culture is its thriving music scene, which pulses through the streets and venues of Saint-Jean-Baptiste. Live performances, whether in intimate bars or bustling outdoor festivals, provide a platform for musicians and performers to share their craft. The neighborhood's venues, known for their warm and welcoming atmospheres, offer a diverse array of sounds, from folk and jazz to indie rock and electronic beats. These performances foster a sense of community and connection, drawing music lovers together in celebration of creativity and expression.

Saint-Jean-Baptiste's culinary scene mirrors its artistic diversity, offering a wide array of flavors and dining experiences that cater to adventurous palates. The neighborhood's restaurants and cafes pride themselves on their innovative menus and commitment to quality, often highlighting locally sourced ingredients and sustainable practices. From cozy bistros serving comfort food to avant-garde eateries pushing the boundaries of culinary art, the district's dining establishments reflect the creativity and passion of their chefs. The emphasis on authenticity and originality ensures that every meal is a delightful exploration of taste and texture.

The community spirit of Saint-Jean-Baptiste is palpable, with residents actively participating in neighborhood events and initiatives that celebrate the district's unique character. Street fairs, art festivals, and cultural gatherings provide opportunities for locals and visitors alike to come together and engage with the vibrant energy of the area. These events not only highlight the talents of local artists and performers but also strengthen the bonds within the community, fostering a sense of belonging and shared purpose.

Education and collaboration are central to the neighborhood's ethos, with workshops, classes, and seminars offering opportunities for learning and growth. These programs, often hosted by local artists and experts, provide a platform for skill-sharing and mentorship, encouraging participants to explore their creative potential. By nurturing talent and fostering connections, Saint-Jean-Baptiste cultivates an environment where innovation and experimentation thrive.

The neighborhood's commitment to sustainability and environmental stewardship is evident in its green initiatives and public spaces. Community gardens, urban agriculture projects, and eco-friendly businesses contribute to the district's reputation as a forward-thinking and responsible community. These efforts not only enhance the quality of life for residents but also inspire others to adopt sustainable practices and consider the impact of their choices on the environment.

Saint-Jean-Baptiste's allure lies in its ability to seamlessly blend the old with the new, creating a dynamic and ever-evolving landscape that invites exploration and discovery. The neighborhood's historic charm, with its cobblestone streets and heritage buildings, provides a picturesque backdrop to the contemporary influences that shape its identity. This juxtaposition of tradition and innovation creates a rich tapestry of experiences that captivate the senses and ignite the imagination.

As evening falls, the streets of Saint-Jean-Baptiste come alive with the sounds of laughter and music, the air filled with the tantalizing aromas of street food and the glow of twinkling lights. The neighborhood's vibrant nightlife offers a myriad of options for entertainment and relaxation, from lively bars and intimate cafes to bustling clubs and performance spaces. Whether you're seeking a quiet drink with friends or an unforgettable night of dancing and music, Saint-Jean-Baptiste provides the perfect setting for memorable experiences.

Saint-Jean-Baptiste, with its bohemian flair and creative energy, offers a unique and enriching experience for those seeking a deeper connection to Quebec City's cultural landscape. The neighborhood's commitment to individuality, diversity, and community creates an environment where creativity and expression are celebrated, inviting all who visit to embrace the spirit of exploration and discovery. In this vibrant district, the possibilities are endless, and the journey is as rewarding as the destination. Here, the heart and soul of bohemian culture thrive, offering a warm welcome to all who seek to experience its magic.

Limoilou: A Blend of Old and New

Limoilou, a neighborhood in Quebec City, is a captivating blend of old-world charm and modern innovation. This area, with its unique character and diverse offerings, provides a fascinating glimpse into the ways in which history and progress can coexist harmoniously. As you wander through its streets, the juxtaposition of the past and present becomes evident, creating a dynamic environment that invites exploration and engagement.

The architecture of Limoilou serves as a testament to its rich history, with its tree-lined avenues showcasing a mix of heritage buildings and contemporary structures. The neighborhood's older homes, with their intricate facades and decorative details, reflect the craftsmanship and architectural styles of a bygone era. These historic residences, often lovingly preserved by their owners, offer a glimpse into the neighborhood's past, evoking a sense of nostalgia and admiration for the skills and artistry of previous generations.

In contrast, Limoilou is also home to modern developments and innovative designs that speak to the area's forward-thinking spirit. Newer constructions, with their sleek lines and sustainable features, demonstrate the neighborhood's commitment to progress and environmental stewardship. These contemporary buildings, often incorporating green technologies and materials, reflect a growing awareness of the need for sustainable urban development. This blend of architectural styles creates a visually striking landscape that embodies the neighborhood's dual identity as both a guardian of tradition and a pioneer of change.

The community's vibrant arts scene further illustrates the harmonious coexistence of old and new in Limoilou. Artisans and creators draw inspiration from the neighborhood's rich history and evolving culture, producing works that resonate with both tradition and innovation. Local galleries and studios provide a platform for artists to showcase their talents, offering visitors the opportunity to engage with a diverse range of artistic expressions. From traditional crafts to contemporary installations, the art of Limoilou reflects the neighborhood's unique character and its ability to adapt and evolve.

The culinary landscape of Limoilou is equally diverse, offering a delicious array of dining experiences that cater to a wide range of tastes and preferences. The neighborhood's eateries, from cozy cafes to upscale restaurants, pride themselves on their innovative menus and commitment to quality. Traditional Quebecois dishes are reimagined with modern twists, while international cuisines are infused with local flavors, creating a fusion of culinary traditions that delights the senses. This emphasis on creativity and authenticity ensures that every meal in Limoilou is a celebration of the neighborhood's rich cultural tapestry.

Public spaces and community initiatives play a crucial role in fostering a sense of connection and collaboration within Limoilou. Parks, gardens, and recreational areas provide residents with opportunities to enjoy the outdoors and engage with their neighbors. These green spaces, thoughtfully integrated into the urban landscape, offer a respite from the hustle and bustle of city life, promoting relaxation and well-being. Community events, such as farmers' markets and cultural festivals, bring people together, strengthening the bonds within the neighborhood and celebrating its diverse heritage.

The entrepreneurial spirit of Limoilou is evident in its thriving local businesses and start-ups, which contribute to the neighborhood's dynamic economy and innovation-driven ethos. Independent shops and boutiques, often family-owned and operated, offer unique products and services that reflect the talents and passions of their owners. This emphasis on supporting local enterprises fosters a sense of pride and loyalty within the community, encouraging residents to shop locally and invest in the neighborhood's continued growth and prosperity.

Education and lifelong learning are key components of Limoilou's identity, with schools, libraries, and community centers providing resources and opportunities for personal and professional development. Workshops, classes, and seminars offer residents the chance to acquire new skills and knowledge, promoting a culture of curiosity and exploration. By nurturing talent and encouraging growth, Limoilou creates an environment where individuals can thrive and contribute to the neighborhood's vibrant cultural landscape.

Limoilou's commitment to sustainability and environmental responsibility is evident in its green initiatives and eco-friendly practices. Community gardens, urban agriculture projects, and recycling programs contribute to the neighborhood's reputation as a leader in sustainable living. These efforts not only enhance the quality of life for residents but also inspire others to adopt environmentally conscious habits and consider the impact of their choices on the planet.

As you explore Limoilou, the neighborhood unfolds as a rich tapestry of experiences, where the past and present converge to create a unique and engaging environment. Whether you're admiring the architecture, savoring a delicious meal, or participating in a community event, Limoilou offers a glimpse into the possibilities that arise when tradition and innovation are embraced in equal measure.

The allure of Limoilou lies in its ability to offer a harmonious blend of old and new, creating an environment where residents and visitors can enjoy the best of both worlds. The neighborhood's commitment to preserving its unique heritage, while embracing new ideas and influences, ensures that it remains a vital and thriving community for generations to come. Here, the spirit of Limoilou is alive and well, offering a warm welcome to all who seek to explore and celebrate the rich history and vibrant traditions that define this remarkable area.

Sillery: Historical Mansions and Riverside Views

Sillery, a distinguished neighborhood in Quebec City, is renowned for its historical mansions and breathtaking riverside views. This elegant area, with its rich heritage and natural beauty, offers a glimpse into the opulence and grandeur of a bygone era while providing a serene escape from the urban bustle. As you meander through its tree-lined streets and verdant landscapes, the charm of Sillery unfolds, revealing a harmonious blend of history, architecture, and nature that captivates the senses.

The historical mansions of Sillery stand as magnificent testaments to the neighborhood's storied past, each with its own unique history and architectural style. These grand residences, built by prominent figures of Quebec's past, reflect the wealth and influence of their original inhabitants. The variety of architectural styles, from neoclassical and Georgian to Victorian and Tudor, showcase the diverse tastes and aspirations of the era. The intricate details and craftsmanship evident in these structures, from ornate facades and elegant verandas to lush gardens and wrought-iron fences, speak to the artistry and dedication of their creators.

Many of these mansions have been meticulously preserved, serving as cultural landmarks and offering a glimpse into the history and lifestyle of Quebec's elite. Some have been repurposed as museums, cultural centers, or luxury accommodations, allowing visitors to step back in time and experience the elegance and refinement of the period. Guided tours provide insight into the history and architecture of these stately homes, sharing stories of the families who once lived there and the events that shaped their lives.

The natural beauty of Sillery further enhances its appeal, with its scenic riverside views offering a tranquil backdrop to the neighborhood's architectural splendor. The St. Lawrence River, with its gentle currents and expansive vistas, provides a picturesque setting for leisurely walks and outdoor activities. Parks and green spaces, thoughtfully integrated into the landscape, offer residents and visitors the opportunity to connect with nature and enjoy the serene ambiance of the area. These spaces, with their well-maintained trails, picnic areas, and recreational facilities, encourage relaxation and contemplation, providing a peaceful retreat from the demands of daily life.

Sillery's commitment to preserving its natural and cultural heritage is evident in its sustainable development practices and community initiatives. Efforts to protect the neighborhood's green spaces and historic sites ensure that the beauty and character of Sillery are preserved for future generations. Community organizations and local government work together to promote awareness and appreciation of the area's unique heritage, fostering a sense of pride and stewardship among residents.

The neighborhood's cultural offerings extend beyond its historical mansions and natural beauty, with a vibrant arts scene that reflects the creativity and diversity of its community. Local galleries and cultural centers provide a platform for artists to showcase their work, offering visitors the chance to engage with a wide range of artistic expressions. From traditional paintings and sculptures to contemporary installations and multimedia projects, the art of Sillery mirrors the neighborhood's rich history and forward-thinking spirit.

Sillery's culinary scene is equally diverse, offering a delectable array of dining experiences that cater to a variety of tastes and preferences. The neighborhood's restaurants, cafes, and bakeries pride themselves on their innovative menus and commitment to quality, often highlighting locally sourced ingredients and sustainable practices. From fine dining establishments offering gourmet cuisine to cozy bistros serving comfort food, the culinary offerings in Sillery reflect the creativity and passion of their chefs. This emphasis on authenticity and originality ensures that every meal is a delightful exploration of flavor and culture.

Education and lifelong learning play a central role in Sillery's community life, with schools, libraries, and cultural institutions providing resources and opportunities for personal and professional development. Workshops, classes, and seminars offer residents the chance to acquire new skills and knowledge, promoting a culture of curiosity and exploration. By nurturing talent and encouraging growth, Sillery creates an environment where individuals can thrive and contribute to the neighborhood's vibrant cultural landscape.

The entrepreneurial spirit of Sillery is evident in its thriving local businesses and start-ups, which contribute to the neighborhood's dynamic economy and innovation-driven ethos. Independent shops and boutiques, often family-owned and operated, offer unique products and services that reflect the talents and passions of their owners. This emphasis on supporting local enterprises fosters a sense of pride and loyalty within the community, encouraging residents to shop locally and invest in the neighborhood's continued growth and prosperity.

The allure of Sillery lies in its ability to offer a harmonious blend of historical grandeur and natural beauty, creating an environment where residents and visitors can enjoy the best of both worlds. The neighborhood's commitment to preserving its unique heritage, while embracing new ideas and influences, ensures that it remains a vital and thriving community for generations to come. Here, the spirit of Sillery is alive and well, offering a warm welcome to all who seek to explore and celebrate the rich history and vibrant traditions that define this remarkable area.

Sillery's charm is further enhanced by its sense of community and connection, with residents actively participating in neighborhood events and initiatives that celebrate the area's unique character. Street fairs, art festivals, and cultural gatherings provide opportunities for locals and visitors alike to come together and engage with the vibrant energy of the area. These events not only highlight the talents of local artists and performers but also strengthen the bonds within the community, fostering a sense of belonging and shared purpose.

As you explore Sillery, the neighborhood unfolds as a rich tapestry of experiences, where the past and present converge to create a unique and engaging environment. Whether you're admiring the architecture, savoring a delicious meal, or participating in a community event, Sillery offers a glimpse into the possibilities that arise when tradition and innovation are embraced in equal measure. Here, the heart and soul of Quebec City's history and culture are celebrated, offering a warm welcome to all who seek to experience its magic.

CHAPTER 7: BEST DAY TRIPS FROM MONTREAL

Mont-Tremblant: Skiing and Outdoor Adventures

Mont-Tremblant, nestled in the heart of the Laurentian Mountains, is a premier destination for skiing and outdoor adventures, offering an invigorating escape from the urban landscape of Montreal. Just a two-hour drive from the bustling city, Mont-Tremblant presents a wonderland of natural beauty and exhilarating activities, making it an ideal day trip for those seeking both thrill and tranquility.

As you approach Mont-Tremblant, the towering peaks and lush forests of the Laurentians come into view, setting the stage for a day filled with exploration and excitement. The resort village, with its charming European-inspired architecture, acts as the gateway to the mountain's diverse offerings. The cobblestone streets, lined with boutiques, cafes, and restaurants, create a vibrant yet cozy atmosphere, inviting visitors to linger and immerse themselves in the alpine charm.

For skiing enthusiasts, Mont-Tremblant is nothing short of paradise. The mountain boasts an impressive array of slopes catering to all skill levels, from gentle beginner trails to challenging expert runs. With over 100 trails spread across four distinct mountain faces, skiers and snowboarders can experience a variety of terrains and stunning vistas. The state-of-the-art lift system ensures quick and easy access to the slopes, allowing for more time spent carving through the powder.

The ski school at Mont-Tremblant is renowned for its expert instructors and comprehensive programs, making it an excellent choice for those new to the sport or looking to refine their skills. Lessons are tailored to individual needs, ensuring a supportive and enjoyable experience on the slopes. For families, the resort offers a range of activities and childcare options, allowing everyone to enjoy their time on the mountain.

Beyond skiing, Mont-Tremblant is a haven for outdoor enthusiasts. The extensive network of trails provides ample opportunities for snowshoeing and cross-country skiing, offering a peaceful and immersive way to experience the winter wonderland. As you traverse these trails, the crisp mountain air and serene landscapes create a profound sense of connection with nature, allowing you to unwind and recharge.

For those seeking a more adrenaline-pumping adventure, the resort offers snowmobiling and ice climbing experiences. These activities provide a unique perspective of the mountain's rugged beauty, challenging participants to push their limits and embrace the thrill of the outdoors. The experienced guides ensure safety and enjoyment, making these adventures accessible to both novices and seasoned adventurers.

As the sun sets and the mountain is bathed in a soft golden glow, Mont-Tremblant transforms into a cozy retreat. The après-ski scene is lively and inviting, with an array of options for relaxation and entertainment. Whether you prefer unwinding in a spa, sipping hot cocoa by a roaring fire, or enjoying live music at a local pub, the village offers a range of experiences to suit every taste.

For those interested in exploring the cultural side of Mont-Tremblant, the village hosts a variety of events and festivals throughout the year. These celebrations showcase the region's rich heritage and vibrant arts scene, offering visitors a chance to engage with the local culture and community. From culinary festivals highlighting regional specialties to music and arts events, there's always something happening in Mont-Tremblant to enrich your visit.

The culinary offerings in Mont-Tremblant are as diverse as its outdoor activities. The village's restaurants and cafes provide a delicious array of dining experiences, from gourmet French cuisine to hearty comfort food. Many establishments emphasize locally sourced ingredients and sustainable practices, ensuring a memorable and conscientious dining experience. Whether you're indulging in a decadent meal at a fine dining restaurant or savoring a casual bite at a cozy bistro, the flavors of Mont-Tremblant are sure to delight.

For those looking to extend their stay, Mont-Tremblant offers a range of accommodations that cater to different preferences and budgets. From luxurious hotels and chalets to charming bed and breakfasts, each option provides a comfortable base from which to explore the mountain and its surroundings. The warm hospitality and personalized service ensure a welcoming and enjoyable experience, making Mont-Tremblant a destination you'll want to return to time and again.

Beyond the winter months, Mont-Tremblant remains a captivating destination, offering a wealth of outdoor activities and natural beauty year-round. In the warmer seasons, the mountain becomes a playground for hikers, mountain bikers, and golfers. The pristine lakes and rivers provide opportunities for kayaking, fishing, and swimming, allowing visitors to connect with the tranquil beauty of the Laurentians.

Mont-Tremblant's commitment to environmental sustainability and conservation is evident in its initiatives to protect and preserve the natural landscape. The resort's efforts to minimize its ecological footprint and promote responsible tourism ensure that this stunning region remains a pristine haven for future generations to enjoy. Visitors are encouraged to participate in eco-friendly practices and explore the natural wonders of Mont-Tremblant with respect and care.

A day trip to Mont-Tremblant offers a perfect blend of adventure and relaxation, providing an escape from the hustle and bustle of Montreal while immersing you in the breathtaking beauty of the Laurentians. Whether you're carving down the slopes, exploring the trails, or simply soaking in the stunning vistas, Mont-Tremblant promises an unforgettable experience that will leave you feeling invigorated and inspired. The mountain's allure lies in its ability to offer something for everyone, making it a must-visit destination for those seeking the ultimate outdoor adventure.

The Laurentians: Nature, Lakes, and Mountains

The Laurentians, a picturesque region north of Montreal, beckon with their stunning landscapes, serene lakes, and majestic mountains. As a haven for nature enthusiasts and adventure seekers alike, the Laurentians provide an ideal day trip destination for those looking to escape the city's hustle and bustle. The journey from Montreal to this breathtaking region is a visual delight as the urban skyline gradually gives way to rolling hills and verdant forests, setting the stage for a day of exploration and discovery.

Upon arriving in the Laurentians, the sheer beauty of the area is immediately apparent. The mountains, draped in lush greenery during the warmer months and blanketed in snow in winter, create a dramatic contrast against the clear blue skies. The air is crisp and invigorating, infused with the earthy scent of pine and the fresh aroma of wildflowers. This natural symphony of sights and scents invites visitors to immerse themselves fully in the experience, leaving the worries of everyday life behind.

Lakes are among the Laurentians' most captivating features, offering a tranquil respite where visitors can unwind and connect with nature. Lac Tremblant, one of the region's largest and most popular lakes, is a prime spot for a variety of water activities. Kayaking, canoeing, and paddleboarding provide an intimate way to explore the lake's crystal-clear waters, while fishing enthusiasts can try their luck at catching trout and bass. For those who prefer a more leisurely experience, a scenic boat tour offers panoramic views of the surrounding mountains and forests, creating a picture-perfect backdrop for relaxation and reflection.

The Laurentians' extensive network of trails makes it a paradise for hikers and nature lovers. The region boasts trails that range from easy, family-friendly walks to challenging treks that reward intrepid adventurers with breathtaking vistas. The Mont-Tremblant National Park, with its diverse ecosystems and abundant wildlife, is a must-visit for those seeking a true wilderness experience. Here, the trails wind through dense forests, alongside rushing rivers, and up to towering peaks, offering opportunities to spot deer, moose, and a variety of bird species in their natural habitat.

Mountain biking is another popular activity in the Laurentians, with numerous trails catering to riders of all skill levels. The region's varied terrain, from rolling hills to rugged mountain paths, provides an exhilarating experience for bikers seeking both challenge and adventure. For a more leisurely ride, the P'tit Train du Nord, a converted railway line, offers a scenic route through charming villages and picturesque landscapes, allowing cyclists to enjoy the beauty of the Laurentians at their own pace.

In the winter months, the Laurentians transform into a snowy wonderland, attracting skiers and snowboarders from near and far. The region is home to several renowned ski resorts, including Mont-Tremblant, which boasts a wide range of slopes and facilities for winter sports enthusiasts. Cross-country skiing, snowshoeing, and ice skating are also popular activities, offering visitors a chance to embrace the magic of winter in the Laurentians' pristine environment.

Beyond outdoor adventures, the Laurentians are rich in cultural experiences and local charm. The region's quaint villages and towns, with their unique blend of history and modernity, provide a glimpse into the area's vibrant heritage. Sainte-Adèle, Val-David, and Saint-Sauveur are just a few of the charming communities where visitors can explore art galleries, craft shops, and local markets. These towns offer a warm welcome and a chance to engage with the local culture, whether through sampling regional delicacies or attending one of the many festivals and events held throughout the year.

The culinary scene in the Laurentians is as diverse as its landscapes, offering a delectable array of dining experiences that cater to all tastes. From cozy cafes serving freshly baked pastries to gourmet restaurants showcasing farm-to-table cuisine, the region's eateries emphasize fresh, locally sourced ingredients. Indulging in a meal at one of these establishments is an opportunity to savor the flavors of the Laurentians, with dishes that reflect the area's rich culinary traditions and innovative spirit.

Accommodation options in the Laurentians are plentiful, ensuring that visitors can find the perfect place to rest and rejuvenate after a day of exploration. From luxurious resorts and charming inns to rustic cabins and cozy bed-and-breakfasts, the region offers a range of choices to suit every preference and budget. Many accommodations feature amenities such as spa services, hot tubs, and panoramic views, allowing guests to unwind and soak in the natural beauty of their surroundings.

Sustainability and conservation are key priorities in the Laurentians, with efforts to preserve the region's natural beauty and promote responsible tourism. Visitors are encouraged to practice Leave No Trace principles, respecting the environment and minimizing their impact on the delicate ecosystems. By fostering a culture of stewardship and appreciation, the Laurentians ensure that its breathtaking landscapes remain a haven for nature lovers and adventurers for generations to come.

A day trip to the Laurentians offers a perfect blend of relaxation, adventure, and cultural enrichment, providing a refreshing escape from the urban pace of Montreal. Whether you're hiking through lush forests, paddling on serene lakes, or savoring the region's culinary delights, the Laurentians promise an unforgettable experience that will leave you feeling inspired and rejuvenated. This enchanting region invites exploration and connection, offering a glimpse into the natural wonders and vibrant culture that make the Laurentians a truly remarkable destination.

Eastern Townships: Wine Tours and Charming Villages

Nestled in the rolling hills southeast of Montreal, the Eastern Townships offer a delightful escape into a world of picturesque landscapes, charming villages, and award-winning vineyards. This region, celebrated for its serene beauty and vibrant culture, makes for an enchanting day trip from the city, inviting visitors to explore its diverse offerings and immerse themselves in its gentle pace of life.

As you venture into the Eastern Townships, the scenery shifts from the urban sprawl to a tapestry of verdant fields, towering maples, and quaint farmsteads. This idyllic setting serves as the perfect backdrop for a day of leisurely exploration, where each turn reveals a new vista or hidden gem. The region's allure lies in its harmonious blend of nature and culture, offering a rich experience for those who seek relaxation and discovery.

One of the Eastern Townships' most enticing attractions is its flourishing wine industry, which has garnered acclaim for both its quality and innovation. The area's vineyards, benefiting from a unique microclimate and fertile soil, produce a diverse array of wines that rival those of more established regions. Wine tours provide an opportunity to taste these local vintages, with many wineries offering guided tastings and tours through their vineyards. This immersive experience not only introduces visitors to the art of winemaking but also offers insight into the region's agricultural heritage and dedication to sustainability.

Participating in a wine tour is as much about the journey as it is about the destination. As you travel from one vineyard to the next, the scenic routes wind their way through rolling countryside, dotted with charming villages and historic sites. These picturesque settlements, with their tree-lined streets and lovingly preserved architecture, invite exploration and engagement with the local culture. Each village has its own unique character and story, providing glimpses into the region's rich history and diverse influences.

A stop in the village of Knowlton, for example, reveals a community steeped in history and brimming with artistic flair. The town's bustling main street is lined with boutique shops, art galleries, and cozy cafes, offering a delightful mix of local crafts and culinary delights. Visitors can stroll along the picturesque shores of Brome Lake or delve into the area's past at the Brome County Historical Society Museum. Knowlton's blend of culture and charm makes it a must-visit destination for those exploring the Eastern Townships.

Another highlight of the region is the village of Sutton, known for its vibrant arts scene and outdoor activities. Nestled at the foot of Mount Sutton, this quaint town offers a wealth of opportunities for adventure and exploration. Hiking and cycling trails abound, inviting visitors to experience the natural beauty of the area firsthand. In the heart of the village, the Sutton Museum and several art galleries showcase the works of local artists, reflecting the community's creative spirit and commitment to cultural preservation.

The Eastern Townships also boast a rich gastronomic tradition, with a focus on farm-to-table dining and locally sourced ingredients. The region's culinary offerings range from artisanal cheeses and charcuterie to gourmet meals crafted by talented chefs. Cozy bistros, elegant restaurants, and bustling farmers' markets provide ample opportunities to savor the flavors of the Eastern Townships, each dish a testament to the region's agricultural bounty and culinary expertise.

In the village of Magog, food enthusiasts can indulge in a diverse array of dining experiences, from lakeside eateries to fine dining establishments. The town's vibrant culinary scene is complemented by its stunning natural surroundings, with the picturesque Lake Memphremagog providing a serene backdrop for leisurely strolls and water activities. Magog's lively atmosphere and diverse offerings make it an ideal stop for those seeking both culinary delights and outdoor adventures.

For those interested in delving deeper into the region's history, the Eastern Townships offer a wealth of historic sites and cultural landmarks. The Abbaye de Saint-Benoît-du-Lac, a stunning Benedictine monastery overlooking Lake Memphremagog, is a testament to the area's religious heritage and architectural splendor. Visitors can explore the abbey's tranquil grounds, attend a service, or sample the monks' renowned cheeses and ciders.

Accommodations in the Eastern Townships range from charming bed and breakfasts to luxurious country inns, ensuring a comfortable and memorable stay for visitors. Many establishments are housed in beautifully restored historic buildings, offering a unique blend of modern amenities and old-world charm. These inviting lodgings provide the perfect base from which to explore the region's attractions, allowing guests to unwind and soak in the serene beauty of their surroundings.

Throughout the Eastern Townships, a strong sense of community and collaboration is evident in the region's numerous festivals and events held throughout the year. From wine and food festivals to music and art fairs, these gatherings celebrate the area's rich cultural heritage and vibrant local talent. Visitors are encouraged to join in the festivities, engaging with the region's diverse traditions and forging connections with its welcoming residents.

The Eastern Townships' commitment to sustainability and environmental stewardship is reflected in its many eco-friendly initiatives and practices. Local businesses and communities work together to promote responsible tourism, ensuring that the region's natural beauty and resources are preserved for future generations. By encouraging visitors to embrace sustainable practices and respect the environment, the Eastern Townships continue to thrive as a model of ecological harmony and cultural richness.

A day trip to the Eastern Townships offers a captivating blend of relaxation, exploration, and cultural enrichment. Whether you're savoring the region's exquisite wines, wandering through its charming villages, or immersing yourself in its vibrant arts scene, the Eastern Townships promise a memorable experience that will leave you feeling rejuvenated and inspired. This enchanting region invites all who visit to pause, reflect, and appreciate the simple pleasures of life, creating lasting memories in a setting of unparalleled beauty and charm.

Oka National Park: Hiking and Beaches

Oka National Park, located just a short drive from Montreal, offers a splendid retreat into nature with its lush forests, serene beaches, and diverse hiking trails. This picturesque park, nestled along the northern shore of the Lake of Two Mountains, provides an ideal setting for outdoor enthusiasts and those seeking a peaceful escape from the city. As you journey towards Oka, the landscapes transition from urban sprawl to verdant greenery, setting the stage for a day filled with exploration and relaxation.

The park's diverse ecosystem is home to a wide array of flora and fauna, offering visitors the chance to connect with nature and discover the unique beauty of the region. With over 23 square kilometers of protected land, Oka National Park is a haven for wildlife, including white-tailed deer, raccoons, and a variety of bird species. This rich biodiversity adds to the park's allure, creating an environment where nature thrives and visitors can immerse themselves in its wonders.

Hiking is one of the most popular activities at Oka National Park, with a network of trails that cater to all levels of experience and fitness. The trails wind through dense forests, open fields, and along the shores of the lake, offering diverse terrains and stunning vistas. The Calvaire d'Oka Trail is particularly well-known, leading hikers to a historic pilgrimage site atop a hill. Along the way, the trail offers breathtaking views of the surrounding landscape, rewarding hikers with a sense of peace and accomplishment.

For those seeking a more leisurely experience, the park's gentle walking paths provide a tranquil setting for a casual stroll. These paths meander through the park's varied environments, allowing visitors to appreciate the natural beauty of Oka at a relaxed pace. Interpretive signs along the trails offer insight into the park's history, ecology, and cultural significance, enriching the experience and fostering a deeper connection with the land.

The beaches at Oka National Park are another major draw, providing a perfect spot for relaxation and recreation. The sandy shores of the Lake of Two Mountains offer a serene setting for sunbathing, picnicking, and swimming, with the gentle waves lapping at the shore creating a soothing soundtrack. The park's beaches are family-friendly, with designated swimming areas and lifeguards on duty during peak seasons, ensuring a safe and enjoyable experience for all.

Water-based activities are plentiful at Oka, with opportunities for kayaking, canoeing, and paddleboarding on the lake's calm waters. Renting equipment is easy and convenient, allowing visitors to explore the lake at their own pace and discover hidden coves and inlets. The tranquil waters provide an ideal setting for both novices and experienced paddlers, with the stunning natural surroundings enhancing the experience.

Cycling enthusiasts will find much to enjoy at Oka National Park, with a network of bike trails that traverse the park's varied landscapes. Whether you're tackling challenging mountain bike paths or enjoying a leisurely ride along paved roads, the park offers routes for all preferences and skill levels. Cycling provides a unique way to explore the park, allowing visitors to cover more ground and experience the diverse environments in a single outing.

For those interested in the cultural and historical aspects of Oka, the park offers several points of interest that reflect the region's rich heritage. The Calvaire d'Oka, a series of historic chapels and crosses, is a testament to the area's spiritual and cultural significance. The site, dating back to the early 18th century, offers a glimpse into the religious traditions and history of the region. Visitors can explore these historic structures and learn about their importance through interpretive displays and guided tours.

Oka National Park is also committed to environmental sustainability and conservation, with efforts to protect its ecosystems and promote responsible tourism. The park's management practices emphasize the importance of preserving the natural environment while providing opportunities for recreation and education. Visitors are encouraged to follow Leave No Trace principles, respecting the park's delicate ecosystems and ensuring their preservation for future generations.

Picnicking is a popular pastime at Oka, with several designated areas providing the perfect setting for a meal amidst nature. The park's picnic sites are equipped with tables, barbecues, and restrooms, offering convenience and comfort for visitors. Sharing a meal with family and friends in the park's tranquil surroundings is a delightful way to unwind and enjoy the beauty of the great outdoors.

Camping is another option for those wishing to extend their stay and fully immerse themselves in the park's natural beauty. Oka National Park offers a range of camping facilities, from rustic tent sites to more comfortable options with amenities. Camping provides an opportunity to experience the park's serene ambiance after the day-trippers have left, with the sounds of nature creating a peaceful backdrop for a night under the stars.

Throughout the year, Oka National Park hosts various events and activities that celebrate the region's natural and cultural heritage. From guided nature walks and birdwatching tours to cultural festivals and workshops, these events offer visitors a chance to engage with the park's diverse offerings and deepen their appreciation for its unique environment.

A day trip to Oka National Park presents a perfect blend of adventure and relaxation, offering a welcome respite from the urban pace of Montreal. Whether you're hiking through its scenic trails, basking on its sandy beaches, or paddling across its tranquil waters, Oka provides a refreshing escape into nature's embrace. This enchanting park invites visitors to explore its beauty, connect with its diverse ecosystems, and create lasting memories in a setting of unparalleled tranquility.

Ottawa: Canada's Capital City

A day trip to Ottawa, the capital city of Canada, offers an enriching journey into the heart of the nation's history, culture, and politics. Just a two-hour drive from Montreal, Ottawa presents a vibrant blend of old-world charm and modern sophistication, making it an ideal destination for those seeking to explore Canada's rich heritage and dynamic urban life.

As you approach Ottawa, the cityscape unfolds with a striking combination of historical landmarks and contemporary architecture. The iconic silhouette of the Parliament Hill complex stands proudly against the skyline, its Gothic Revival style and storied history drawing visitors from near and far. This seat of Canadian democracy offers a glimpse into the nation's political life and serves as a symbol of its enduring legacy.

One of the highlights of any visit to Ottawa is a tour of Parliament Hill. The guided tours provide insight into the workings of the Canadian government, allowing visitors to explore the House of Commons, the Senate, and the Library of Parliament. The tours are both informative and engaging, offering a deeper understanding of Canada's political system and the historical events that have shaped the nation. In the summer months, the Changing of the Guard ceremony adds a touch of pageantry and tradition, delighting spectators with its precision and grandeur.

Beyond the political sphere, Ottawa boasts a wealth of cultural attractions that reflect the diverse fabric of Canadian society. The National Gallery of Canada, with its extensive collection of Canadian and Indigenous art, is a must-visit for art enthusiasts. The striking architecture of the gallery, including the iconic glass tower, offers a visual treat even before stepping inside. The gallery's exhibitions highlight Canada's artistic heritage, showcasing works from renowned artists such as the Group of Seven and Emily Carr, alongside contemporary pieces that challenge and inspire.

Ottawa is also home to the Canadian Museum of History, located just across the Ottawa River in Gatineau. This impressive museum offers a comprehensive look at Canada's past, with exhibits that delve into the lives of Indigenous peoples, the impact of European colonization, and the evolution of Canadian society. The museum's Grand Hall, with its awe-inspiring collection of totem poles and Indigenous art, provides a powerful introduction to the nation's rich cultural heritage.

For those interested in science and innovation, the Canada Science and Technology Museum offers an interactive experience that engages visitors of all ages. The museum's exhibits explore the history of Canadian innovation, from the development of the transcontinental railway to the modern advances in space exploration. This hands-on museum is perfect for families, offering a fun and educational outing that sparks curiosity and discovery.

Ottawa's vibrant neighborhoods add to the city's appeal, each offering a unique blend of history, culture, and local flavor. ByWard Market, one of the city's oldest and most popular districts, is a bustling hub of activity with its eclectic mix of shops, restaurants, and markets. Visitors can explore the lively streets, sampling local delicacies such as BeaverTails and artisanal cheeses, or browse the stalls for handmade crafts and souvenirs.

The Rideau Canal, a UNESCO World Heritage site, is another of Ottawa's treasured landmarks. In the warmer months, the canal offers a picturesque setting for leisurely strolls, cycling, or boat tours. As winter descends, the canal transforms into the world's largest skating rink, inviting visitors to glide along its frozen surface amidst the enchanting winter scenery. This seasonal transformation adds a magical touch to the Ottawa experience, making it a must-see attraction regardless of the time of year.

For nature enthusiasts, Ottawa's numerous parks and green spaces provide a refreshing escape from the urban environment. Gatineau Park, just a short drive from the city center, offers a stunning array of trails and vistas, with opportunities for hiking, cycling, and picnicking. The park's diverse landscapes, from dense forests to serene lakes, create a tranquil retreat where visitors can connect with nature and unwind.

Ottawa's culinary scene reflects the city's multicultural identity, offering a diverse array of dining experiences that cater to all tastes. From fine dining establishments that showcase Canadian cuisine with a modern twist to cozy pubs serving hearty fare, the city's restaurants provide a delicious exploration of flavors and traditions. Local specialties, such as poutine and tourtière, offer a taste of Canadian comfort food, while international influences add a global flair to the dining landscape.

Throughout the year, Ottawa hosts a variety of festivals and events that celebrate the city's cultural diversity and artistic spirit. The Canadian Tulip Festival, held each spring, transforms the city into a vibrant sea of color, with millions of tulips blooming in parks and gardens. This celebration of beauty and renewal draws visitors from around the world, offering a stunning spectacle and a reminder of Ottawa's international connections.

For those interested in music and the arts, the Ottawa Jazz Festival and the Ottawa International Animation Festival provide opportunities to experience world-class performances and cutting-edge creativity. These events, along with numerous others, contribute to the city's dynamic cultural scene, offering something for everyone to enjoy.

In traveling to Ottawa, visitors are invited to explore the rich tapestry of Canada's capital city, discovering its historical landmarks, cultural treasures, and vibrant neighborhoods. This day trip offers a perfect blend of education, entertainment, and relaxation, providing a deeper understanding of the nation's past and present. Whether you're touring the iconic Parliament Hill, skating on the Rideau Canal, or savoring the diverse culinary offerings, Ottawa promises an unforgettable experience that captures the essence of Canada.

Île Sainte-Hélène and Île Notre-Dame: Parks and Historical Sites

Situated in the heart of the Saint Lawrence River, Île Sainte-Hélène and Île Notre-Dame form a captivating duo of islands that offer a perfect day trip for those seeking a blend of nature, history, and recreation. Easily accessible from Montreal, these islands are part of Parc Jean-Drapeau, a sprawling urban park that provides an escape into scenic landscapes and a rich tapestry of cultural and historical attractions.

As you arrive on Île Sainte-Hélène, you're greeted by the verdant expanse of the island, which boasts a variety of walking trails, picnic areas, and lush gardens. The island's natural beauty invites exploration, with paths that meander through wooded areas and open spaces, offering stunning views of the city skyline. This tranquil setting provides a refreshing contrast to the urban buzz, making it a favorite spot for locals and visitors alike.

Île Sainte-Hélène is home to several notable historical sites, each offering a glimpse into the island's storied past. One of the most prominent landmarks is the Stewart Museum, housed in a 19th-century British military depot. The museum's extensive collection of artifacts and exhibits brings to life the history of New France and the colonial era, providing a fascinating journey through time. Visitors can explore the museum's exhibits, which include military artifacts, historical documents, and interactive displays, all of which illuminate the island's strategic importance throughout history.

Nearby, the Fort de l'Île Sainte-Hélène stands as a testament to the island's military significance. Originally constructed in the early 19th century to defend Montreal against potential American invasions, the fort offers a rich historical narrative. Guided tours of the fort allow visitors to delve into its history, exploring the barracks, powder magazine, and ramparts. These tours provide a deeper understanding of the island's role in shaping the region's history and its military heritage.

Île Sainte-Hélène is also home to La Ronde, Quebec's largest amusement park, which offers a thrilling array of rides and attractions for visitors of all ages. From adrenaline-pumping roller coasters to family-friendly rides, La Ronde provides an exciting day of fun and entertainment. The park's vibrant atmosphere and diverse offerings make it a popular destination for families and thrill-seekers alike, ensuring a day filled with laughter and adventure.

Crossing the bridge to Île Notre-Dame, visitors are greeted by a different kind of landscape, one characterized by expansive green spaces and sophisticated attractions. This island was artificially created for Expo 67, the World's Fair held in Montreal, and has since become a hub of cultural and recreational activities.

One of Île Notre-Dame's standout features is the Montreal Casino, housed in the former French and Quebec pavilions of

Expo 67. This architectural marvel offers a world-class gaming experience, with a wide array of table games, slot machines, and entertainment options. The casino's lively atmosphere and stunning river views make it a must-visit destination for those looking to try their luck or enjoy an evening of entertainment.

For nature lovers, Île Notre-Dame boasts the verdant beauty of the Floralies Gardens, a magnificent collection of themed gardens and floral displays. Originally created for the 1980 International Floralies horticultural exhibition, these gardens provide a serene escape into nature's splendor. Visitors can wander through the diverse gardens, each showcasing a different theme or style, and enjoy the vibrant colors and fragrant blooms that create a feast for the senses.

The island is also home to the Circuit Gilles Villeneuve, a renowned Formula 1 racing track that hosts the annual Canadian Grand Prix. When not in use for racing events, the track is open to the public, offering a unique venue for cycling, inline skating, and leisurely walks. The track's picturesque setting along the river and its proximity to lush parkland make it a popular destination for outdoor enthusiasts seeking a unique and scenic route.

In addition to its recreational offerings, Île Notre-Dame provides ample opportunities for relaxation and leisure. The island's beaches offer a tranquil retreat, where visitors can unwind on the sandy shores, swim in the refreshing waters, or enjoy a picnic amidst the island's natural beauty. These serene spots are perfect for those looking to escape the city's hustle and bustle and enjoy a day of sun and sand.

Both Île Sainte-Hélène and Île Notre-Dame are committed to sustainability and environmental conservation, with initiatives aimed at preserving the islands' natural beauty and promoting eco-friendly practices. Visitors are encouraged to respect the islands' ecosystems, practicing Leave No Trace principles and supporting efforts to protect the environment.

Throughout the year, Parc Jean-Drapeau hosts a variety of events and festivals that celebrate the islands' cultural diversity and vibrant spirit. From music festivals and art exhibitions to sporting events and family-friendly activities, these gatherings offer a dynamic array of experiences that engage and entertain visitors of all ages. Participating in these events provides an opportunity to connect with the local community and experience the islands' lively atmosphere firsthand.

A day trip to Île Sainte-Hélène and Île Notre-Dame offers a delightful blend of history, nature, and recreation, providing a perfect escape from the urban pace of Montreal. Whether you're exploring the islands' historical sites, enjoying the thrill of La Ronde, or relaxing on the sandy beaches, these islands promise a memorable experience that captures the essence of Montreal's unique charm. This enchanting destination invites visitors to discover its treasures, creating lasting memories in a setting of unparalleled beauty and cultural richness.

CHAPTER 8: BEST DAY TRIPS FROM QUEBEC CITY

Île d'Orléans: Agricultural Heritage and Scenic Drives

Just a short drive from Quebec City lies Île d'Orléans, an island that embodies the pastoral charm and rich agricultural history of the region. This jewel of the Saint Lawrence River offers visitors a delightful retreat into a world of scenic beauty and cultural heritage, where time seems to stand still amidst the fields, orchards, and charming villages. A day trip to Île d'Orléans provides an opportunity to explore the island's diverse landscapes, savor its renowned local produce, and experience the warmth and hospitality of its communities.

The journey to Île d'Orléans begins with a drive across the Pont de l'Île, a bridge that connects the island to the mainland. As you cross the bridge, the hustle and bustle of the city gradually give way to the serene vistas of rolling hills and verdant farmland. This transition sets the tone for a day of leisurely exploration, where each bend in the road reveals new scenes of rustic beauty. The island's landscape is a patchwork of fertile fields, orchards heavy with fruit, and vineyards that stretch towards the horizon, all framed by the shimmering waters of the Saint Lawrence.

The charm of Île d'Orléans is encapsulated in its six picturesque villages, each with its own unique character and history. As you meander along the island's scenic routes, these villages beckon with their quaint stone houses, historic churches, and inviting artisan shops. Sainte-Pétronille, located at the island's western tip, offers breathtaking views of Quebec City and Montmorency Falls. This village, with its elegant homes and lush gardens, has long been a retreat for artists and poets, drawn by its tranquil ambiance and inspiring vistas.

Continuing around the island, the village of Saint-Jean boasts a rich maritime heritage, reflected in its charming waterfront and historic shipyard. Here, visitors can explore the Maison Drouin, one of the oldest houses on the island, which offers a glimpse into the daily life of early settlers. The house, meticulously preserved, provides an intimate look at the island's history and the resilience of its inhabitants.

Île d'Orléans is famed for its agricultural bounty, and no visit would be complete without indulging in the island's culinary delights. The island's fertile soil and temperate climate make it an ideal location for growing a wide variety of produce, from apples and strawberries to grapes and vegetables. Farm stands and markets dot the island, offering fresh, locally grown produce that captures the essence of the season. Visitors can sample the island's famous cider, wine, and ice cider, all crafted from the fruits of its orchards and vineyards.

The island's culinary tradition extends beyond its produce to its artisanal products and gourmet offerings. From creamy cheeses and charcuterie to handmade chocolates and preserves, Île d'Orléans is a paradise for food lovers. Many local producers welcome visitors for tastings and tours, providing a behind-the-scenes look at their craft and a chance to savor the flavors of the island.

One of the island's most cherished culinary traditions is its maple syrup production, a practice that dates back to the time of the early settlers. The island's sugar shacks offer a sweet taste of this heritage, with opportunities to learn about the syrup-making process and enjoy traditional maple treats. Visiting a sugar shack is a delightful experience, offering a blend of education and indulgence that appeals to all ages.

For those seeking outdoor adventure, Île d'Orléans offers a range of activities that showcase its natural beauty. Cycling is a popular way to explore the island, with a network of scenic routes that wind through its villages and countryside. The island's gentle terrain and picturesque landscapes make it an ideal destination for cyclists of all levels, providing a leisurely way to discover its hidden gems.

In addition to cycling, the island's shores offer opportunities for kayaking and canoeing, allowing visitors to experience the tranquil beauty of the Saint Lawrence River. Paddling along the island's coastline provides a unique perspective on its landscapes, with the chance to spot local wildlife and enjoy the peaceful rhythm of the water.

Throughout the year, Île d'Orléans hosts a variety of festivals and events that celebrate its cultural and agricultural heritage. From harvest festivals and music concerts to art exhibitions and culinary workshops, these events offer a lively and engaging experience for visitors. Participating in these gatherings provides an opportunity to connect with the island's vibrant community and immerse oneself in its traditions.

Accommodations on Île d'Orléans range from charming bed and breakfasts to cozy inns, many of which are housed in historic buildings that reflect the island's architectural heritage. Staying overnight allows visitors to fully immerse themselves in the island's serene ambiance and enjoy the tranquility of its rural landscapes. The island's accommodations offer a warm welcome and a chance to experience the genuine hospitality of its residents.

Île d'Orléans is also committed to preserving its natural and cultural heritage, with initiatives that promote sustainable tourism and environmental stewardship. Visitors are encouraged to respect the island's ecosystems and support local businesses, ensuring that the island's beauty and traditions are preserved for future generations.

A day trip to Île d'Orléans offers a captivating journey into the heart of Quebec's agricultural heritage and scenic beauty. Whether you're exploring its charming villages, savoring its culinary delights, or enjoying its outdoor activities, the island promises a memorable experience that captures the essence of rural Quebec life. This enchanting destination invites visitors to slow down, savor the moment, and discover the simple pleasures of life amidst its idyllic landscapes.

Charlevoix: Whale Watching and Mountain Views

Nestled between the majestic Laurentian Mountains and the vast St. Lawrence River, Charlevoix offers a breathtaking retreat for those seeking awe-inspiring natural beauty and unforgettable wildlife encounters. Just a couple of hours northeast of Quebec City, this region provides a day trip filled with scenic drives, thrilling whale watching, and the serene presence of towering peaks. Charlevoix is a place where nature sings its most melodious tunes, inviting visitors to lose themselves in its harmonious landscapes.

The drive to Charlevoix sets the stage for an enchanting day, as the road winds along the St. Lawrence River, offering glimpses of its expansive waters and the distant silhouette of the mountains. The region's charm lies in its rugged terrain, shaped by ancient glaciers and dramatic geological events that have given rise to its unique topography. This geological wonderland captivates with its rolling hills, deep valleys, and jagged cliffs, creating a natural canvas that delights the senses.

One of the most exhilarating experiences in Charlevoix is whale watching, an activity that draws enthusiasts and nature lovers from around the world. The nutrient-rich waters of the St. Lawrence Estuary create a prime feeding ground for a variety of whale species, including the majestic blue whale, the acrobatic humpback, and the playful beluga. Several operators offer whale watching tours departing from towns like Tadoussac and Baie-Sainte-Catherine, providing an up-close look at these magnificent creatures in their natural habitat.

Boarding a boat for a whale watching excursion is an adventure in itself. The crisp air and gentle sway of the boat as it navigates the estuary set the mood for an unforgettable encounter. As the boat ventures into deeper waters, the anticipation builds, and the first sight of a whale breaking the surface is a moment of pure magic. The sight of these gentle giants, their sheer size and grace, inspires a profound sense of awe and reminds us of the wonders of the natural world.

While the whales are undoubtedly the stars of the show, the estuary is also home to a rich diversity of marine life, including seals, porpoises, and an array of seabirds. The knowledgeable guides on board provide fascinating insights into the ecology of the region, enhancing the experience with stories and facts about the marine environment. These tours offer an educational journey that deepens appreciation for the delicate balance of the ecosystem and the importance of conservation efforts.

Beyond the waters, Charlevoix's landscapes beckon with their rugged beauty and panoramic vistas. The region's mountainous terrain offers ample opportunities for hiking and exploration, with trails that cater to all levels of fitness and experience. The Acropole des Draveurs trail in the Hautes-Gorges-de-la-Rivière-Malbaie National Park is a challenging yet rewarding hike that takes adventurers to the summit, where sweeping views of the surrounding valleys and peaks unfold in all directions.

The trail's ascent is a journey through diverse ecosystems, from lush forests to alpine meadows, each offering its own distinct beauty. The invigorating climb, punctuated by the sounds of rustling leaves and distant bird calls, culminates in a breathtaking panorama that rewards the effort with an unparalleled sense of accomplishment. Standing atop the Acropole des Draveurs, one can feel the timeless power of the mountains and the tranquility they exude.

For those seeking a more leisurely experience, the Charlevoix region offers scenic drives that showcase its natural splendor. The Route du Fleuve, or River Road, is a particularly picturesque route that winds along the coast, passing through charming villages and offering stunning views of the river and mountains. This drive is a journey through time, with quaint homes, historic churches, and artisanal shops dotting the landscape, each with its own story to tell.

The village of Baie-Saint-Paul, known for its vibrant arts scene, is a must-visit along the way. This charming town is a haven for artists and creatives, with galleries and studios displaying an array of works that capture the essence of the region. Visitors can wander the streets, browse the galleries, and perhaps find a piece of art that resonates with their own experience of Charlevoix.

Culinary delights are another highlight of a day trip to Charlevoix, with the region's fertile land and bountiful waters providing a rich tapestry of flavors. From fresh seafood and succulent meats to artisanal cheeses and handcrafted chocolates, the local cuisine reflects the bounty of the land and sea. Restaurants and bistros throughout the region offer dishes that showcase the best of local produce, often accompanied by spectacular views that enhance the dining experience.

Charlevoix's commitment to sustainable tourism and environmental stewardship is evident in its many eco-friendly initiatives and practices. The region's natural beauty is preserved through efforts to protect its ecosystems and promote responsible tourism. Visitors are encouraged to tread lightly, respect the environment, and support local businesses that prioritize sustainability.

Throughout the year, Charlevoix hosts a variety of festivals and events that celebrate its cultural heritage and natural wonders. From music festivals and art exhibitions to outdoor adventures and culinary experiences, these events offer a dynamic and engaging way to connect with the region's vibrant community. Participating in these gatherings provides an opportunity to immerse oneself in the local culture and traditions, creating lasting memories and connections.

A day trip to Charlevoix offers a harmonious blend of adventure, relaxation, and discovery, providing a perfect escape into the heart of nature's beauty. Whether you're marveling at the graceful dance of whales, hiking through majestic landscapes, or savoring the region's culinary delights, Charlevoix invites you to embrace its wonders and find inspiration in its enchanting vistas. This captivating destination promises an experience that lingers in the heart and mind, a testament to the timeless allure of the natural world.

Saint-Anne-de-Beaupré: Pilgrimage and Architecture

Saint-Anne-de-Beaupré, a quaint town nestled along the banks of the St. Lawrence River, offers a day trip filled with spiritual reflection and architectural marvels. Just a short drive from Quebec City, this destination is renowned for its famous basilica, drawing pilgrims and tourists alike to its sacred grounds. The town, with its serene atmosphere and picturesque surroundings, provides a perfect setting for a journey that nourishes both the soul and the senses.

The main attraction in Saint-Anne-de-Beaupré is undoubtedly the Basilica of Sainte-Anne-de-Beaupré, a stunning masterpiece of religious architecture. As you approach the basilica, its twin spires and grand facade rise majestically against the sky, inviting visitors to explore its hallowed halls. The basilica, dedicated to Saint Anne, the patron saint of Quebec, has been a site of pilgrimage for centuries, attracting millions seeking solace, healing, and inspiration.

Upon entering the basilica, one is immediately struck by the sense of awe and reverence that permeates the space. The interior of the basilica is a work of art in itself, with intricate mosaics, stained glass windows, and ornate sculptures that tell the stories of faith and devotion. The craftsmanship and attention to detail evident in every corner reflect the deep spiritual significance of the place, making it a powerful experience for visitors of all beliefs.

The basilica's history is as fascinating as its architecture. The original chapel, built in the 17th century, was a humble wooden structure that quickly gained a reputation for its miraculous healings. Over the years, the site evolved, with several iterations of the church being constructed to accommodate the growing number of pilgrims. The current basilica, completed in the early 20th century, stands as a testament to the enduring legacy of Saint Anne and the unwavering faith of those who come to seek her intercession.

In addition to the basilica itself, the surrounding grounds offer a variety of sites for reflection and exploration. The Way of the

Cross, a series of outdoor stations depicting the Passion of Christ, provides a meditative path for pilgrims to walk, each station offering a moment of contemplation and prayer. The gardens, with their vibrant flora and peaceful ambiance, invite visitors to pause and appreciate the beauty of creation.

The Cyclorama of Jerusalem, located near the basilica, offers a unique and captivating experience. This massive panoramic painting, over a century old, depicts the crucifixion of Jesus in stunning detail. The 360-degree artwork transports viewers to ancient Jerusalem, providing a vivid and immersive glimpse into biblical history. The Cyclorama is a remarkable feat of artistry, showcasing the skill and dedication of its creators and leaving a lasting impression on all who visit.

Beyond its religious significance, Saint-Anne-de-Beaupré boasts a rich cultural heritage that reflects the region's history and traditions. The town's charming streets are lined with quaint shops and cafes, offering local crafts, souvenirs, and culinary delights. Visitors can savor traditional Quebecois fare, sample regional specialties, or simply enjoy a leisurely stroll through the town's picturesque surroundings.

The natural beauty of the area enhances the experience, with the sweeping vistas of the St. Lawrence River and the rolling hills of the Laurentians providing a breathtaking backdrop. Outdoor enthusiasts can take advantage of the nearby trails and parks, exploring the region's diverse landscapes through hiking, cycling, or even a scenic drive. The fresh air and tranquility of the countryside offer a welcome respite from the bustle of city life.

Throughout the year, Saint-Anne-de-Beaupré hosts a variety of events and festivals that celebrate its spiritual and cultural heritage. From religious processions and music concerts to art exhibitions and community gatherings, these events provide an opportunity to connect with the local community and experience the town's vibrant spirit. Participating in these festivities offers a deeper understanding of the traditions and values that define this unique destination.

For those seeking a deeper spiritual experience, the town offers retreats and workshops that provide opportunities for reflection and personal growth. These programs, often held at the basilica or nearby centers, offer a chance to engage with like-minded individuals and explore themes of faith, healing, and renewal. Whether you are on a personal pilgrimage or simply seeking a moment of peace, these offerings provide a meaningful way to connect with the spiritual heart of Saint-Anne-de-Beaupré.

Accommodations in the area range from cozy bed and breakfasts to comfortable inns, many of which offer a warm and welcoming atmosphere that reflects the hospitality of the region. Staying overnight allows visitors to fully immerse themselves in the town's serene ambiance, providing a chance to unwind and reflect on the day's experiences. The local accommodations often feature stunning views of the surrounding landscapes, enhancing the sense of tranquility and relaxation.

Saint-Anne-de-Beaupré's commitment to preserving its cultural and spiritual heritage is evident in its efforts to maintain and promote the town's historical sites and traditions. Visitors are encouraged to support local businesses and initiatives, ensuring that the town's legacy is preserved for future generations. The community's dedication to sustainability and stewardship is a testament to its respect for the past and its vision for the future.

A day trip to Saint-Anne-de-Beaupré offers a unique and enriching experience, blending spiritual reflection, architectural wonder, and cultural exploration. Whether you are drawn by the basilica's sacred aura, the town's historical charm, or the natural beauty of the region, this destination promises a memorable journey that touches the heart and soul. Saint-Anne-de-Beaupré invites visitors to discover its treasures, fostering connections and creating lasting memories in a place where history, faith, and beauty converge.

Parc National de la Jacques-Cartier: Nature at Its Finest

A short drive from Quebec City, Parc National de la Jacques-Cartier offers an escape into the heart of nature's magnificence. This national park, renowned for its dramatic landscapes and abundant wildlife, is a haven for outdoor enthusiasts and those seeking tranquility in the embrace of towering mountains and lush valleys. As you venture into the park, the world slows down, inviting you to immerse yourself in the beauty and serenity that define this natural wonder.

The journey to Parc National de la Jacques-Cartier is an experience in itself, with the road winding through picturesque countryside and hinting at the grandeur that awaits. Upon arrival, the sight of the Jacques-Cartier River carving its way through a deep glacial valley sets the stage for a day of exploration and discovery. The river, with its crystal-clear waters and gentle rapids, is a central feature of the park, offering a dynamic backdrop to the diverse activities available.

Hiking is one of the most popular ways to experience the park's natural beauty, with a network of trails catering to all levels of fitness and expertise. Whether you're an experienced hiker seeking a challenging ascent or a beginner looking for a leisurely walk, the park offers a trail that suits your needs. The Les Loups trail, known for its sweeping views, takes hikers through dense forests and along ridges that provide panoramic vistas of the valley below. The trail's moderate difficulty and the stunning scenery it offers make it a favorite among visitors.

For those who prefer a gentler pace, the Sentier de la Rivière offers a more relaxed exploration along the river's edge. This trail, suitable for families and casual walkers, meanders through lush forests and offers numerous spots to pause and enjoy the tranquility of the surroundings. The soothing sounds of the river, combined with the dappled sunlight filtering through the trees, create a peaceful ambiance that invites reflection and relaxation.

Water enthusiasts will find plenty to enjoy in the park, with the Jacques-Cartier River providing opportunities for canoeing, kayaking, and fishing. Paddling along the river allows visitors to experience the park from a unique perspective, as the gentle current carries them past towering cliffs and verdant forests. The river's calm stretches and occasional rapids offer a mix of serenity and excitement, making it suitable for both novice and experienced paddlers.

Fishing in the park is a popular activity, with the river and its tributaries teeming with brook trout and other species. Anglers can try their luck from the riverbanks or venture into the water for a more immersive experience. The tranquility of the river, combined with the thrill of the catch, creates a rewarding experience that connects visitors with the natural world.

Wildlife observation is another highlight of Parc National de la Jacques-Cartier, with the park's diverse ecosystems supporting a wide array of animal species. From moose and deer to beavers and various bird species, the park offers ample opportunities to observe wildlife in their natural habitat. Early morning and late afternoon are ideal times for wildlife spotting, as many animals are most active during these hours. Visitors are encouraged to bring binoculars and a camera to capture the beauty and diversity of the park's inhabitants.

The park's commitment to conservation and education is evident in its efforts to protect its natural resources and promote sustainable tourism. Interpretive programs and guided tours provide visitors with insights into the park's ecology, geology, and history, enhancing their understanding and appreciation of the environment. These educational opportunities offer a deeper connection to the park and its mission to preserve its natural beauty for future generations.

Picnic areas and designated rest spots throughout the park provide ideal settings for enjoying a meal amidst nature's splendor. Visitors can relax and recharge while taking in the breathtaking views, with the sounds of the river and the calls of the forest as their backdrop. These moments of pause allow for reflection and appreciation of the park's serene ambiance.

Throughout the year, Parc National de la Jacques-Cartier hosts a variety of events and activities that celebrate the changing seasons and the park's natural wonders. From guided snowshoe tours in winter to stargazing events in summer, these activities offer unique ways to experience the park and connect with the rhythms of nature. Participating in these events provides a deeper understanding of the park's ecological significance and the importance of its preservation.

Accommodations near the park range from cozy cabins to campsites, offering visitors the opportunity to extend their stay and fully immerse themselves in the natural environment. Staying overnight allows for a more relaxed exploration of the park, with the chance to experience the tranquility of its landscapes at dawn and dusk. The local accommodations often feature stunning views and a warm, welcoming atmosphere that enhances the overall experience.

The park's location, close to Quebec City, makes it an accessible and convenient day trip for those seeking a retreat into nature. The journey to and from the park provides an opportunity to enjoy the scenic beauty of the region, with the drive itself offering glimpses of the landscapes that define this part of Quebec. The proximity to the city allows for a seamless blend of urban and natural experiences, providing a perfect balance for travelers.

A day trip to Parc National de la Jacques-Cartier offers an opportunity to reconnect with nature and experience the beauty and tranquility of its landscapes. Whether you're hiking through lush forests, paddling along the river, or observing wildlife in their natural habitat, the park promises a memorable journey that refreshes the spirit and inspires a deep appreciation for the natural world. This stunning destination invites visitors to explore its wonders, creating lasting memories in a setting of unparalleled beauty and serenity.

Wendake: Indigenous Culture and History

Nestled on the outskirts of Quebec City, Wendake offers a captivating journey into the rich history and vibrant culture of the Huron-Wendat Nation. This unique destination invites visitors to explore the indigenous heritage that has shaped the region for centuries, providing an enriching experience that combines history, tradition, and community. A day trip to Wendake is an opportunity to engage with the living culture of the Huron-Wendat people and to gain a deeper understanding of their enduring legacy.

Arriving in Wendake, the sense of community and cultural pride is immediately palpable. The village is a harmonious blend of tradition and modernity, where historical landmarks and contemporary spaces coexist, reflecting the dynamic nature of indigenous identity. The heart of Wendake is the Huron-Wendat Museum, a cultural institution dedicated to preserving and sharing the history and traditions of the Huron-Wendat Nation. The museum offers a comprehensive introduction to the community's past, present, and future, showcasing artifacts, exhibits, and multimedia presentations that tell the story of the Huron-Wendat people.

As you explore the museum, the depth and richness of Huron-Wendat culture come to life through the carefully curated displays. From intricate beadwork and traditional clothing to tools and ceremonial objects, each artifact offers a glimpse into the daily life, artistry, and spirituality of the Huron-Wendat people. The exhibits highlight the resilience and adaptability of the community, emphasizing their ability to maintain cultural continuity while embracing change.

One of the museum's most compelling features is its focus on storytelling, an integral aspect of Huron-Wendat culture. Through oral histories, recorded narratives, and interactive displays, visitors are invited to hear the voices of the past and present, connecting with the personal stories that form the fabric of the community. These narratives provide insight into the values, beliefs, and experiences that have shaped the Huron-Wendat identity, fostering a deeper appreciation for their cultural heritage.

Adjacent to the museum is the Onhoüa Chetek8e Traditional Huron Site, an immersive experience that transports visitors to a reconstructed 17th-century Huron-Wendat village. Here, the traditional longhouses, smokehouses, and artisan workshops offer a tangible connection to the community's ancestral way of life. Guided tours provide an in-depth exploration of the site, with knowledgeable interpreters sharing insights into the daily practices, social structures, and spiritual beliefs of the Huron-Wendat people.

The traditional site also offers hands-on activities that allow visitors to engage directly with Huron-Wendat crafts and skills. From traditional cooking demonstrations to workshops on beadwork and woodcarving, these activities provide an opportunity to learn from skilled artisans and gain a deeper understanding of the techniques and artistry that define Huron-Wendat craftsmanship. Participating in these activities fosters a sense of connection and appreciation for the community's creative expression.

Wendake is also home to a vibrant culinary scene that showcases the flavors and ingredients central to Huron-Wendat cuisine. Local restaurants and eateries offer dishes that blend traditional recipes with contemporary influences, reflecting the community's innovative approach to food and hospitality. Visitors can savor a variety of dishes featuring game meats, wild berries, and indigenous herbs, each offering a taste of the region's rich culinary heritage. Dining in Wendake is a sensory experience that celebrates the bounty of the land and the creativity of its people.

Throughout the year, Wendake hosts a variety of cultural events and festivals that celebrate indigenous traditions and showcase the talents of the community. These gatherings offer a lively and engaging experience for visitors, providing an opportunity to witness traditional music, dance, and storytelling performances. From powwows and craft markets to seasonal celebrations and cultural workshops, these events offer a dynamic and immersive way to connect with the Huron-Wendat culture.

The community's commitment to cultural preservation and education is evident in its efforts to promote sustainable tourism and foster cross-cultural understanding. Visitors are encouraged to engage with the community in a respectful and meaningful way, supporting local businesses and initiatives that prioritize cultural integrity and environmental stewardship. Wendake's approach to tourism emphasizes the importance of building authentic relationships and fostering mutual respect, ensuring that the community's cultural heritage is shared and celebrated responsibly.

Accommodations in Wendake range from cozy inns to modern hotels, many of which offer a warm and welcoming atmosphere that reflects the hospitality of the Huron-Wendat people. Staying overnight provides an opportunity to fully immerse oneself in the community's cultural ambiance, with the chance to experience the tranquility of the village and its surroundings. The local accommodations often feature elements of indigenous design and décor, enhancing the overall experience and creating a sense of place that is both comforting and inspiring.

The natural beauty of the Wendake area adds to the allure of the visit, with its lush forests, rolling hills, and scenic waterways providing a stunning backdrop for outdoor exploration. Hiking and nature trails invite visitors to discover the region's diverse landscapes, offering a peaceful retreat into nature and a chance to connect with the land that has sustained the Huron-Wendat people for generations. The harmony between the community and its environment is a testament to the deep respect and reverence that define Huron-Wendat culture.

A day trip to Wendake offers a profound and enriching experience, inviting visitors to engage with the history, culture, and community of the Huron-Wendat Nation. Whether exploring the museum, participating in traditional crafts, or savoring indigenous cuisine, Wendake provides a unique opportunity to connect with the living heritage of the Huron-Wendat people. This vibrant destination celebrates the resilience and creativity of its community, fostering connections and creating lasting memories in a place where culture, history, and hospitality come together in harmony.

Baie-Saint-Paul: Art Galleries and Local Charm

Baie-Saint-Paul, a picturesque town nestled in the heart of the Charlevoix region, offers a delightful escape into a world where art and nature converge. Known for its charming streets and vibrant arts scene, this destination invites visitors to explore a tapestry of creativity and local charm just an easy drive from Quebec City. A day trip to Baie-Saint-Paul promises a feast for the senses, with its kaleidoscope of galleries, boutiques, and stunning natural landscapes that inspire artists and travelers alike.

As you approach Baie-Saint-Paul, the lush rolling hills and meandering river views create a serene backdrop that sets the tone for the day ahead. This town, cradled by the Laurentian Mountains and the St. Lawrence River, captivates with its scenic beauty and welcoming atmosphere. Its natural landscapes have long drawn artists seeking to capture its ethereal light and vivid colors on canvas, and today, it stands as a beacon of creativity and cultural expression.

The heart of Baie-Saint-Paul is its bustling arts scene, with an array of galleries showcasing works from both established and emerging artists. The town is renowned for its role in the emergence of the "Group of Seven," an influential group of Canadian landscape painters, and its artistic legacy continues to flourish. As you stroll through the streets, you'll find galleries tucked into historic buildings, each offering a unique perspective on the vibrant local art scene.

One of the most notable stops is the Galerie d'Art Iris, a cornerstone of Baie-Saint-Paul's artistic community. This gallery, housed in a charming heritage building, displays a diverse collection of contemporary art, including paintings, sculptures, and mixed media works. The curated exhibitions highlight the dynamic range of artistic talent in the region, providing visitors with a captivating glimpse into the creative spirit that defines Baie-Saint-Paul.

Another must-visit is the Maison Otis, a cultural hub that combines art, history, and hospitality under one roof. Originally a 19th-century inn, Maison Otis now functions as a gallery space featuring rotating exhibitions from local artists. Its historic charm, coupled with the innovative works on display, creates an inviting atmosphere that encourages exploration and reflection.

For those interested in a more interactive experience, Baie-Saint-Paul offers a variety of art workshops and classes that cater to all skill levels. Whether you're a seasoned artist or a curious beginner, these opportunities provide a chance to engage with the creative process and learn new techniques. Local artists often lead these sessions, sharing their expertise and passion for their craft, and offering insight into the artistic traditions of the region.

Baie-Saint-Paul's artistic appeal extends beyond its galleries, permeating the town's vibrant streets and public spaces. The town itself is a living canvas, with murals adorning building facades and sculptures dotting its parks and squares. These public artworks celebrate the community's cultural heritage and serve as a testament to its commitment to fostering creativity and artistic expression.

As you wander through Baie-Saint-Paul, the town's culinary scene beckons with its array of local flavors and gastronomic delights. The region's fertile land and abundant waters provide a rich palette of ingredients, inspiring chefs to create dishes that reflect the bounty of the Charlevoix region. From cozy cafes and bistros to upscale dining establishments, the town offers a diverse range of culinary experiences that satisfy both the palate and the soul.

A visit to the local farmers' market provides a chance to sample the region's finest produce, cheeses, and artisanal products. The market, bustling with vendors and locals, offers a glimpse into the community's agricultural roots and its dedication to sustainable practices. As you stroll through the stalls, the vibrant colors and enticing aromas create an inviting atmosphere that celebrates the flavors of the region.

Beyond its artistic and culinary offerings, Baie-Saint-Paul is a gateway to the natural beauty that defines the Charlevoix region. Outdoor enthusiasts will find plenty to explore, with hiking and cycling trails that wind through the surrounding hills and along the river. These trails offer a chance to experience the breathtaking landscapes that have inspired countless artists, providing a sense of peace and connection to the natural world.

The Rivière du Gouffre, which flows through Baie-Saint-Paul, offers opportunities for kayaking and canoeing, allowing visitors to experience the town from a different perspective. Paddling along the gentle currents, surrounded by the lush greenery and distant mountains, provides a moment of tranquility and reflection. The river's serene beauty and the rhythmic sound of the water create a soothing backdrop for a day of exploration.

Throughout the year, Baie-Saint-Paul hosts a variety of cultural events and festivals that celebrate its artistic heritage and community spirit. From music festivals and theater performances to art fairs and culinary events, these gatherings offer a dynamic and engaging way to experience the town's vibrant culture. Participating in these events provides a deeper understanding of the traditions and values that define Baie-Saint-Paul, creating lasting memories and connections.

Accommodations in Baie-Saint-Paul range from charming bed and breakfasts to boutique hotels, each offering a warm and welcoming atmosphere that reflects the town's hospitality. Staying overnight allows visitors to fully immerse themselves in the town's ambiance, with the chance to experience its charm and beauty at a more leisurely pace. The local accommodations often feature artistic touches, enhancing the overall experience and creating a sense of place that is both comforting and inspiring.

Baie-Saint-Paul's commitment to preserving its cultural and natural heritage is evident in its efforts to promote sustainable tourism and foster community engagement. Visitors are encouraged to support local businesses and initiatives that prioritize environmental stewardship and cultural integrity. The town's approach to tourism emphasizes the importance of building authentic relationships and fostering mutual respect, ensuring that its legacy is preserved for future generations.

A day trip to Baie-Saint-Paul offers a harmonious blend of art, nature, and local charm, providing a perfect escape into the heart of creativity and inspiration. Whether you're exploring the town's galleries, savoring its culinary delights, or discovering its natural landscapes, Baie-Saint-Paul invites you to embrace its wonders and find inspiration in its captivating beauty. This enchanting destination promises an experience that lingers in the heart and mind, a testament to the timeless allure of art and community.

CONCLUSION: YOUR PERFECT ADVENTURE AWAITS

Recap of Key Highlights

A journey through the captivating landscapes and cultural treasures surrounding Quebec City reveals an impressive array of experiences, each offering a unique glimpse into the diverse tapestry that defines this region. From the majestic architecture of Saint-Anne-de-Beaupré to the vibrant artistic community of Baie-Saint-Paul, these day trips invite exploration and discovery, encouraging a deeper connection with the natural beauty and rich heritage that characterize Quebec.

Saint-Anne-de-Beaupré stands as a beacon of spirituality and architectural grandeur. The basilica, with its intricate mosaics and soaring spires, draws pilgrims and visitors seeking moments of reflection and awe. The history of this sacred site, intertwined with tales of miraculous healings and enduring faith, adds layers of depth to the experience. Exploring the basilica's hallowed halls and serene gardens offers a profound sense of peace and inspiration, making it a must-visit destination for those seeking both spiritual and cultural enrichment.

In contrast, the natural splendor of Parc National de la Jacques-Cartier offers an immersive escape into the heart of the wilderness. The park's rugged landscapes, shaped by glacial valleys and the winding Jacques-Cartier River, provide a breathtaking backdrop for outdoor adventures. Whether hiking through dense forests, paddling along the river, or observing wildlife in their natural habitat, visitors are invited to reconnect with nature and embrace the tranquility it offers.

The park's commitment to conservation and education further enhances the experience, fostering a deeper appreciation for the environment and its preservation.

Wendake, with its vibrant indigenous culture and rich history, offers a journey into the living heritage of the Huron-Wendat Nation. The Huron-Wendat Museum and the Onhoüa Chetek8e Traditional Huron Site provide immersive experiences that celebrate the community's traditions, artistry, and resilience. Engaging with the stories, crafts, and culinary delights of Wendake offers a unique opportunity to connect with the cultural heart of the region, fostering understanding and respect for the indigenous legacy that continues to thrive.

The artistic charm of Baie-Saint-Paul captivates with its flourishing arts scene and picturesque surroundings. The town's galleries, workshops, and public art installations reflect its creative spirit, offering inspiration to artists and visitors alike. The culinary offerings, rooted in the region's agricultural bounty, provide a taste of local flavors and traditions. Exploring Baie-Saint-Paul's vibrant streets and natural landscapes reveals a harmonious blend of art, culture, and nature, creating a memorable experience that lingers in the mind.

Each of these destinations, with their unique highlights and attractions, contributes to a richer understanding of the Quebec region. The diverse experiences available, from spiritual reflection and cultural engagement to outdoor adventure and artistic exploration, offer something for every traveler. The proximity of these destinations to Quebec City makes them accessible and convenient, allowing for seamless integration into any itinerary.

In reflecting on these experiences, it becomes evident that the true essence of the region lies in its ability to inspire, connect, and enrich. The natural beauty, cultural heritage, and community spirit encountered on these day trips create a tapestry of memories and impressions that resonate long after the journey ends. Whether seeking solace in a sacred space, adventure in the wilderness, or connection with cultural traditions, these highlights offer a gateway to the heart of Quebec.

The journey through Quebec's surrounding treasures invites reflection and appreciation for the myriad facets that define this remarkable region. Each destination, with its distinct character and offerings, contributes to a deeper understanding of the area's cultural and natural richness. As travelers explore these highlights, they are encouraged to embrace the diversity and beauty that make Quebec an unforgettable destination, fostering connections and creating lasting memories in a place where history, culture, and nature converge harmoniously.

Final Travel Tips and Advice

Embarking on a journey through the captivating surroundings of Quebec City calls for careful preparation and a spirit of adventure. As you prepare to explore the diverse array of day trips and destinations, a few practical travel tips and advice can enhance your experience and ensure a seamless and memorable adventure.

First and foremost, planning your itinerary with flexibility in mind is crucial. While it's tempting to map out every moment, allowing for spontaneity can lead to unexpected discoveries and experiences that enrich your journey. Research the destinations you're interested in, but remain open to the possibility of stumbling upon hidden gems along the way. Local festivals, unique eateries, and lesser-known attractions often provide some of the most memorable experiences, so embrace the opportunity to deviate from your original plan when curiosity strikes.

Transportation is a key consideration when exploring the regions surrounding Quebec City. Whether you choose to rent a car, use public transportation, or join guided tours, each option offers its own set of benefits. Renting a car provides the greatest flexibility, allowing you to explore at your own pace and venture off the beaten path. If you prefer a more relaxed approach, public transportation or guided tours can offer convenient and stress-free alternatives, with the added benefit of local insights and expertise. Whichever mode of transport you choose, ensure you have a reliable map or GPS system to navigate the area's charming yet sometimes intricate roadways.

Packing wisely is another essential element of a successful day trip. The varied climates and activities in the Quebec region mean that dressing in layers is a practical strategy. From the cool breezes along the St. Lawrence River to the warm interiors of art galleries and museums, layers allow you to adjust to changing temperatures comfortably. Sturdy footwear is also a must, especially if you plan to explore natural parks or engage in outdoor activities. A small daypack stocked with essentials like water, snacks, and a portable phone charger will keep you prepared for whatever the day may bring.

Language can play a significant role in your travel experience, as French is the predominant language in Quebec. While many locals speak English, making an effort to communicate in French, even at a basic level, can enhance your interactions and show respect for the local culture. Simple greetings, expressions of gratitude, and polite inquiries can go a long way in fostering positive connections with the people you meet. Consider carrying a pocket-sized phrasebook or language app to help bridge any linguistic gaps.

When it comes to dining, Quebec is a food lover's paradise, with its rich culinary traditions and innovative chefs offering a delectable array of flavors. To make the most of your culinary adventures, seek out local specialties and regional dishes that showcase the area's unique ingredients. From hearty tourtières and savory poutines to sweet maple-infused treats, the region's cuisine is a reflection of its diverse cultural influences and abundant natural resources. Don't hesitate to ask locals for recommendations, as they often have insider tips on the best eateries and markets.

Respecting the environment and local communities is paramount when traveling, particularly in areas known for their natural beauty and cultural heritage. Practice sustainable tourism by minimizing waste, conserving resources, and supporting local businesses that prioritize eco-friendly practices. Whether you're hiking through a national park or visiting an indigenous community, show respect for the land and its people by adhering to guidelines and seeking

211

permission when necessary. These actions not only protect the environment but also contribute to the preservation of cultural traditions and the well-being of local communities.

Capturing your travel memories is an integral part of the journey, and Quebec's picturesque landscapes and vibrant culture provide endless opportunities for photography. To capture the essence of your experiences, consider varying your shots to include wide-angle views of stunning vistas, candid moments of local life, and detailed images of artistic and architectural elements. While it's tempting to document every moment, remember to balance photography with the simple act of being present and fully immersed in your surroundings.

Safety is always a priority when traveling, and a few precautions can ensure a worry-free experience. Keep copies of important documents such as your passport, identification, and travel insurance, and store them separately from the originals. Stay informed about local conditions, weather forecasts, and any advisories that may affect your travel plans. Trust your instincts and exercise common sense, particularly when exploring unfamiliar areas or engaging in new activities.

Finally, embrace the spirit of curiosity and openness that travel inspires. Each destination around Quebec City offers its own unique charm and opportunities for learning and growth. Engage with locals, ask questions, and seek to understand the history and culture that shape the region. By approaching your travels with an open mind and a willingness to learn, you'll enrich your experience and create lasting memories that extend beyond the physical journey.

As you prepare for your adventure, these travel tips and advice serve as a guide to navigating the diverse and captivating landscapes of Quebec. From the bustling streets of charming villages to the tranquil beauty of natural parks, the region's rich tapestry of experiences awaits your discovery. With thoughtful preparation and a spirit of adventure, your journey promises to be a rewarding exploration of the beauty, culture, and diversity that define Quebec.

Inspiration for Your Next Visit

Quebec City and its enchanting surroundings offer an endless array of experiences that captivate the hearts and minds of travelers. From the cobblestone streets steeped in history to the breathtaking natural landscapes, this region is a wellspring of inspiration. As you contemplate your next visit, consider the myriad ways in which Quebec can ignite your imagination and enrich your journey.

The historic charm of Old Quebec is a perfect starting point, with its European flair and timeless elegance. Strolling through the fortified walls of this UNESCO World Heritage site, you can almost hear the echoes of centuries past. The majestic Château Frontenac stands as a sentinel over the city, a testament to its grand history and architectural splendor. Imagine wandering through the narrow alleyways, each twist and turn revealing new secrets and stories waiting to be discovered. The vibrant Place Royale, with its colorful facades and cobblestone square, invites you to pause and soak in the atmosphere, perhaps with a steaming cup of café au lait in hand.

Venture beyond the city walls, and the serene beauty of the Île d'Orléans awaits. Often referred to as the "Garden of Quebec," this island is a haven for those seeking tranquility and inspiration. Picture yourself cycling along its scenic roads, the gentle breeze carrying the scent of apple orchards and blooming lilacs. The island's charming villages, each with its own unique character, offer glimpses into rural life and the region's rich agricultural heritage. Capture the essence of Île d'Orléans in your mind's eye, a tableau of rolling fields, historic farmsteads, and the glistening expanse of the St. Lawrence River.

For those drawn to the majesty of nature, the Charlevoix region beckons with its dramatic landscapes and abundant wildlife. Envision yourself hiking through the verdant trails of the Hautes-Gorges-de-la-Rivière-Malbaie National Park, the towering cliffs and rushing river creating a symphony of sights and sounds. The rugged beauty of this region, shaped by ancient geological forces, inspires a sense of awe and wonder. Allow yourself to be immersed in its splendor, where each vista is more breathtaking than the last, and every moment is an invitation to connect with the natural world.

The artistic soul finds its muse in Baie-Saint-Paul, a town renowned for its vibrant arts scene and creative energy. Imagine exploring the galleries and studios, each one a treasure trove of artistic expression and innovation. The town's picturesque setting, nestled between mountains and river, serves as a constant source of inspiration for artists and visitors alike. As you wander through its streets, the colorful murals and public art installations remind you of the transformative power of creativity and the boundless possibilities it holds.

Cultural encounters await in Wendake, where the rich traditions of the Huron-Wendat Nation offer a window into the indigenous heritage of Quebec. Picture yourself participating in a traditional craft workshop, your hands guided by skilled artisans as you learn the techniques passed down through generations. The stories shared by community members, whether through music, dance, or oral history, provide a deeper understanding of their enduring legacy. Wendake invites you to engage with its culture in a meaningful way, fostering connections and appreciation for the diversity that enriches the region.

The culinary landscape of Quebec is a feast for the senses, offering a delectable fusion of flavors that reflect its diverse cultural influences. Envision yourself savoring a meal at a local bistro, the menu a celebration of seasonal ingredients and innovative techniques. From classic French cuisine to indigenous-inspired dishes, the region's gastronomic offerings are a testament to its rich culinary heritage. Each bite tells a story, connecting you to the land, its people, and the traditions that define Quebec's food culture.

As you dream of your next visit, consider the seasonal wonders that transform Quebec into a living canvas throughout the year. In winter, the city becomes a snow-draped wonderland, inviting you to embrace the joys of ice skating, snowshoeing, and sipping hot chocolate by a crackling fire. The Quebec Winter Carnival, with its ice sculptures and lively festivities, adds a touch of magic to the season. Spring breathes new life into the region, as cherry blossoms and tulips burst into bloom, painting the landscape with vibrant colors. Summer's warmth invites outdoor adventures, from kayaking along the river to exploring lush gardens and parks. Autumn, with its fiery foliage and crisp air, offers a perfect backdrop for scenic drives and harvest festivals.

Quebec's festivals and events provide endless inspiration, celebrating the region's culture, history, and creativity. Imagine attending the Festival d'été de Québec, where world-class musicians and performers light up the stage against the backdrop of the historic city. The New France Festival transports you back in time, with costumed reenactments and lively parades that bring history to life. Each event is an opportunity to immerse yourself in the spirit of Quebec, experiencing the joy and camaraderie that define its vibrant community.

As you ponder the possibilities, let your imagination be your guide. Whether you're drawn to the region's history, natural beauty, artistic expression, or culinary delights, Quebec offers a wealth of experiences that inspire and delight. Each visit is a chance to create new memories, discover hidden treasures, and connect with the essence of this remarkable region. Embrace the adventure, and let Quebec's charm and wonder captivate your heart and soul.

BONUS 1: ESSENTIAL PHRASES FOR YOUR DAILY TRAVEL NEEDS IN CANADA

BONUS 2: PRINTABLE TRAVEL JOURNAL

BONUS 3: 10 TIPS "THAT CAN SAVE THE DAY" ON YOUR CANADIAN TRIP

Printed in Great Britain
by Amazon

57757285R00121